A Full House of Growing Pains

A Full House
of Growing Pains

A Hollywood mother's journey ...

by Barbara Cameron

with Lissa Halls Johnson

Bridge-Logos
Orlando, Florida 32822

Bridge-Logos

Orlando, FL 32822 USA

Full House of Growing Pains
by Barbara Cameron
with Lissa Halls Johnson

Printed in the United States of America.

Library of Congress Catalog Card Number: 2006928295
International Standard Book Number 0-88270-189-4

Cover photo of Kirk Cameron © Jim Britt
Cover photo of Candace Cameron by Paul Fenton Photography
Cover photo of the Cameron family by Tim Walton
Cover photo of Barbara Cameron by Carol J. Scott of CJ Studios

Cover design by Tobias Outerwear for Books

dedication

For Robert

Thank you for your patience and understanding
through the ups and downs of our life together.
I look forward to many more wonderful years with you.

For my children,
Kirk, Bridgette, Melissa, and Candace

Thank you for forgiving me for the decisions I made that were
hurtful to you. May this book give you a glimpse of who I was
then and who I am today. You have all made me proud
to be your mother. Thank you for all of your love and support
in helping me write this book.

For Chelsea and Kirk

Thank you for helping me see this book through to completion
with all your beautiful details. Chelsea, thank you for your
beautiful heart, encouragement, and support of this book.

Contents

chapter 1

Happily Ever After

S*oon.*

Was I, Barbara Cameron, good wife and mother, really going to go through with this? I pushed back the thoughts of what I *should* be doing. I knew I should feel ashamed, that I shouldn't do this. Instead, I remembered how good it felt when Steve smiled at me. How wonderful it was that his dark brown eyes lit up when I came into the room.

It's okay.

Looking out the window, I made sure my husband Robert's truck was gone. I didn't have much time to get ready. I had scooted Melissa and Bridgette out the door to friends' houses. They had looked at me as though I'd lost my mind. I almost never let them go to anyone's house. But today was different. I didn't want them here.

What they didn't know was that I hadn't lost my mind. I'd finally gotten a grasp of it. For too many years I'd let Robert walk all over me. For too many years I'd let his hurtful words crush my heart and tear me to pieces. Too long I'd felt like the real me was almost invisible to my own husband. Too many times I wanted to cry when he, just being friendly, turned his back on me to sit in rapt attention as some gorgeous woman captivated him while I sat like a fat, ugly lump behind him. For too many years I'd let him dictate to me what I should feel and how I should think about any issue at hand.

This afternoon I was going to take a step toward regaining myself. *Steve.*

How had I been so lucky to meet such an incredible man? A smile moved from my face to my heart, melting every part of me.

"Hi, Barb, how ya doing?" he'd say every day on the *Growing Pains* set.

"Better," I'd answer, hoping he'd hear what I didn't say out loud, but inferred.

Better because you are here. Better because you see me.

"Good." His smile bathed my torn soul. "When are you going to go into business for yourself? You'd be a great agent, you know."

"Not yet. Too much going on with the kids." I pretended that what he said didn't matter much. When in reality, I took his words in and let them heal the places Robert had wounded. Steve thought I had potential. Steve believed in me. Steve enjoyed being around me. Steve liked *me.* I didn't feel invisible around Steve.

How long had it been since Robert seemed to *really* like me? Fifteen years? Eighteen? Had he forgotten the sandy, wet girl he had been smitten with when we met on the beach? The girl who blew him away at the front door, her hair in curls, sundress showing off her tan?

Had he forgotten how he had loved me so much? How excited he was not only to find a girl to marry, but one who wanted to marry him so badly she'd proposed to him?

What did it matter? Our marriage had been hard for so long. Robert made it clear from day one that he was the master of the house and no woman would ever, *ever* control him. From day one, he discouraged me from having strong opinions. He wouldn't tell me where he was going to take me to dinner, because he didn't want to hear me make any comments about his choice—even positive ones. He'd gone from suffering under a controlling mother to being hyper-controlling himself, and wanting to be sure his wife didn't control him at all.

In the beginning, I loved all that about him. I loved that he was so strong and sure. I didn't have to do the hard work of making decisions. He happily made them, and I happily accepted them.

I tidied up the kitchen and tried to tell myself that Robert wasn't all bad. After all, without him, I wouldn't be able to manage the kids' acting careers. The family would have needed me at home. Robert carried half the household load without complaint. Without him, the non-acting daughters, Bridgette and Melissa, would have little parental attention. He helped Bridgette and Melissa do their homework. He washed the dishes.

But he can be so mean.

Yeah, he helped the girls, but he yelled at them and said hurtful things when they couldn't understand their homework.

Truth of the matter was, I was miserable—and had been for far too many years. I'd told myself I'd leave Robert after the kids were gone. For their sake I'd wait until the last one turned eighteen or left home. But why wait? Surely it was okay with God if I was happy *now*. Isn't that why I met Steve? Wasn't Steve a sign that God wanted to give me a way out of this verbally abusive marriage? Steve was an incredible gift from God. And today, we were going to move from on-set flirting to an off-set date. And what a date it was going to be! My husband may have repressed me, but I'm still a woman. I knew what the pull of chemistry feels like. I knew the silent messages shouted in body language. He cared for me; there was no doubt about that.

This might be official date number one, but it felt as though we'd been dating for some time. In a way, perhaps, we had … just surreptitiously, under the watchful eyes of the cast and crew.

I took the Nordstrom's dress bag from my closet. Lifting the plastic, I gazed at the new pantsuit. I pictured myself in it. Pictured *him* seeing me in it. His broadening smile. His chestnut brown eyes, taking in every inch of me, so pleased at what he saw.

I'd dreamed of having a first real kiss for months now. I knew it would be tender, gentle, inviting.

I slipped the clothing off the hanger and laid the pieces on the bed.

Robert made me feel insignificant as a woman. Unimportant. Barely sufficient. I knew weight was important to him. My goodness, he kept track of the girls' weight on a chart, weighing them every Sunday. He doled out food as though it were important for them to stay at some expected ideal. I couldn't imagine what he thought about me. Never slender, but never fat. Just an endless chubbiness.

Until now.

I put on the periwinkle slacks that clung to my slender figure in soft, fluid fabric. The matching jacket and white top looked stunning. The top clung to my curves, enticing another look. The blue in my eyes deepened. I turned in front of the mirror. I'd worked so hard to lose these twenty pounds—for Steve.

Funny how you can do things easily for someone who appreciates your hard work.

"You look fabulous today, Barb."

I lived for those words. I'd given up hearing Robert say them. But to hear them from Steve …

My blond hair fell onto my shoulders. I grabbed a handful and held it up, turning from side to side, deciding. Up or down?

Down. It looks more beach casual.

I slipped on black flats and tip-toed into the bathroom. I dug into my makeup bag and removed mascara, shadow, eyebrow pencil, and lipstick. I paused at the foundation, and then let it go. I reapplied my makeup, finishing with the coral lipstick, smoothing the color on. I pressed my lips together and stood back.

My heart reacted, jump-starting to triple time.

Is this really happening?

I'd never been a girl to seek anything outside the norm. Yet I felt something missing in my life as wife and mother. It wasn't that I hadn't liked being a mother. I couldn't pinpoint the emptiness. I couldn't believe I used to try to drum up fulfillment and excitement by spending hours doing macramé, then hosting home parties. No, I had a new life now. The life everyone dreamed of. Hollywood. Glamour. Glitz. Being written about in magazines. Being on talk shows. Rubbing shoulders with some stars and being friends—yes, *friends*—with others. I tried to hide it, but it was tremendously exciting. I was *known* in Hollywood. I had my own money. My own connections. A nice, new, silver BMW convertible. I could go do this dangerous thing because I wasn't little Barbara, Robert's quiet wife anymore. No, I was Barbara *Cameron*. Teen heartthrob Kirk Cameron's mom. Yes, I was the Mike Seaver's real-life mom. I was also the mom of the sweet, lovable Candace Cameron, who played DJ Tanner on *Full House*.

And there is a man who cares about me.

There are defining moments in everyone's life. A moment when everything changes. For some, the moment happens *to* them. A car accident. A medical diagnosis. A death. I was tired of letting life happen *to* me. Tired of letting Robert choose. Tired of his insensitive comments that everyone laughed at but me. Tired of feeling like the brunt of a joke. Of being silent everywhere Robert and I went together because he dominated the conversation. It used to be okay, because I knew he was so smart and I was so dumb. But now I wanted to be at least a little bit smart. And Steve obviously thought I was.

I knew I wasn't innocent in the mess my marriage had become. I'd contributed. I'd yelled. I'd kept quiet when maybe I should have said something. But nothing I said to Robert seemed to change anything. And I didn't know how to say it anyway. I didn't know how to make him understand that I wanted to be *one* with him. And now it just felt like it was too late. I was so tired of fighting. Tired of trying.

No more!

Today I planned to take my life into my hands. I would show strength by taking a huge stride toward freedom and by doing something different. As I met Steve on the beach, I would define my own eventful moment that would change my life forever.

I shivered with excitement.

Taking up my handbag, I stepped into the warm California sunshine.

chapter 2

Good Beginnings

I was raised to be a good girl. And I *was* a good girl. Unlike some kids, I really *wanted* to be good. I didn't rebel, but obeyed and respected my parents. I told the truth almost all the time. I didn't drink or do drugs. I didn't sleep around; Robert was the only man I'd ever been intimate with. I was known as a prude, or called goody-two shoes by some less prone to want to be good. I made far more good choices than bad ones.

Like many kids who want to be good, I was influenced in part by my desire-to-please personality, in part by my strict parental upbringing, and in part by the church they dropped us off at every Sunday.

My parents raised my four siblings and me to know right from wrong, to respect our elders, and to follow the "Golden Rule." They taught us that we should never lie or steal, and should always obey our parents.

My father enforced these moral codes by instilling fear of retribution. I could swear he had a way of spying on us and discovering us even when we did the smallest thing wrong. My father not only had eyes in the back of his head, he had eyes and ears everywhere— more like the Phantom in the classic *Phantom of the Opera* story. I

Opposite page: *Barbara* (in foreground) *with sisters Joanne and Lynda and Grandaddy Murphy.*

feared my father's punishment, which involved spanking, grounding, and/or taking away privileges. Even his stern words and glare to match were enough to send one quivering into goodness.

Mom enforced the moral codes by pointing to Dad as the disciplinarian. Whenever we were out of line, my mother would say, "Just wait 'til your father gets home!" None of us wanted to hear those words or wait those dragging hours to find out what Dad would do once he heard about our misdeeds.

They linked their training with the teachings of the church and Vacation Bible School. There I heard lots of wonderful, exciting Bible stories. Grown-ups who looked very important taught me about God being big and wise and powerful and perfect. And also that He was kind of like my dad—that He could see you from anywhere and would punish you if you sinned. When they spoke of God, my strongest visual image was of my dad's face, hovering kind of like the green vaporous image of the wizard in *The Wizard of Oz*.

My teachers also taught me about Jesus loving everybody and living on earth and dying on a cross. They said it was very important for me to accept Jesus into my heart and be saved from hell. I added up all those pieces of information and, as a good little girl should, believed in each of them and practiced them all.

Once I told a friend that I was afraid of God because if I wasn't a good girl, I would go to hell. He told me that it wasn't true. How could a God that loved me want to send me to Hell? I didn't know what to think about that idea, but knew in my heart that there was a place called Hell and I didn't want to go there. So I set out to understand what I needed to do to avoid hell. As far as I knew, I had covered all the bases: believe in God and ask Jesus into my heart and be forgiven for my sins.

I had a limited understanding of the concept of sin. I thought it meant that I shouldn't steal or tell lies, and if I did, to quickly say, "I'm sorry," and that it was really no big deal because God would just forgive me. Then I went out and repeated the cycle all over again. But really, compared to lots of other kids I knew, I wasn't so bad. Maybe I made some mistakes, but mostly, it seemed, I got it right.

I loved going to church, but not the process of getting there. Before we could leave, Dad lined us up to be sure that we were dressed appropriately. I swallowed hard during lineup, sometimes holding my breath, trying hard to stand still. Inside, I quivered, waiting for something—anything—to be wrong. And it often was. If my belt was too big or too tight, or my petticoat was too full, I would have to go back to my room and change—fast. I was usually in tears before Sunday school ever started.

Once at church, however, I loved to sing songs, listen to the Bible stories, watch the flannel board people, do the crafts, and see my friends. Most of all, I looked forward to refreshment time with cookies and juice.

Sunday school always ended too soon. I sat low in the car, kicking the seat in front of me, dread creeping inside, shutting down every playful desire I had. I knew that after a quick lunch, we would work all afternoon on detested chores. We cleaned our rooms or weeded and mowed the lawn—chores I knew most other people did on Saturdays.

As years passed and miserable Sunday added to miserable Sunday, I decided that when I left home, I would happily choose different activities for that day. Church and chores would not be among them.

For the most part, I had a happy childhood. My three sisters and baby brother squabbled over the usual stupid things. We laughed, teased each other, and hung tight. Dad worked hard in construction, while Mom followed in her mother's footsteps by being a fabulous housewife. Mom and Dad loved each other and loved us. Their stories were typically American, setting the stage for their children's families to be typically American as well.

Mom and Dad met in high school. As the stereotype continues, Jeanne Murphey was a cheerleader and Frank Bausmith was a football star. Dad was blond and handsome. Mom was one of those pin-up beauties like Marilyn Monroe, only with dark hair. Before they married, Dad joined the 4th Marine division out of Camp Lejeune, North Carolina. From there, he was shipped off to fight in the Pacific islands. Mom and Dad wrote emotion-packed letters back and forth for two-and-a-half years. Dad started writing his letters with the greeting, "Dear Jeanne." It wasn't long before it developed into "My Darling Jeanne."

After they married, they settled in New Jersey where they built their family, child by loved child. Growing up in the Bausmith home was never dull! Instilled within us were the qualities and values of hard work, good morals, hospitality, and above all else, the importance of family.

Mom basically raised us, and her kids were her entire world. She loved being a mom and continually searched for inventive ways to entertain us kids. During the summer, she encouraged us to set up stands on the sidewalk in front of our house to sell Kool-Aid, gum, and candy. We looked forward to peddling our goods every chance we got, learning all about costs and profit. (We especially liked the profits—no matter how meager.)

Mom spent the months before Christmas stockpiling little gifts for us so on that special day we each had a tower of presents to open. No matter that tearing off the wrapping might reveal socks or underpants. Mom loved giving lots of gifts to open, and we kids loved having them!

Mom knitted and sewed—talents she learned from her mother. Both these women could entertain at the drop of a hat. Our Nana worked as a waitress in a tea room and made hors d'oeuvres for a banquet caterer. While she lived with us she kept her culinary skills sharp and made eating fun by doing things like cutting our sandwiches in fancy shapes.

We kids entertained guests with our perceived talents as actors and vocalists. All our costumes came from Mom's closet. She seemed to delight in letting us be so creative.

Dad taught us all to be self-sufficient and to take charge. My sisters and I were extraordinarily physically strong. I, to my humiliation, was known as the chubby one. When I look back at photos taken of my childhood, I can't imagine why people told me that. My sister Lynda was extremely thin. Compared to her, we were all chubby. But that word clung to me like a baby monkey that won't let go of its mother. It colored how I saw myself for decades to come. Linked with the label of chubby came the idea that a chubby girl is also dim-witted, a bit dull and inadequate as a person. I bought into all those characteristics and believed wholeheartedly that I was shamefully all of them.

When I was with my sister Joanne and my dad, I had confidence and loved trying new adventures. Together we did some awesome things. We liked to wrestle, play tag football at the park, and be anywhere Dad would go with us—whether it involved the guy stuff in the outdoors, or sprawling on the living room carpet to watch TV.

Sometimes it's odd to me how much we loved Dad and craved his attention, even though he could be rather harsh. For example, we all took turns saying a standard grace over our meals. "God is great. God is good. Let us thank Him for our food. Amen." Joanne didn't speak clearly, so when it was her turn to pray the standard prayer, she'd say what sounded like, "Let us thankin' for our food." Dad would bop her on her head. "It's thank *Him*, Joanne, not thankin'. Do it again."

Again and again she would try, and after each failed effort, Dad would bop her on the head. The food cooled while the rest of us sat silent and still in our places, heads bowed to distance ourselves from Joanne's humiliation.

Dad was the king of the home, or the silver-backed gorilla, as Robert later called him, and subtly made that clear. If a child reached with her fork to pierce the last piece of meat, Dad's fork pierced it first.

On the other hand, Dad worked very hard and always provided us with a beautiful home, food on the table, and vacation every summer with the extended family to the Jersey shore. The big, burly football player had kept his physique through hard construction work and could be either a cuddly teddy bear, or just a bear, depending on his mood, or which one of us had disappointed him.

Water seemed to play a big part in our growing-up years. We loved those vacations to the Jersey shore. With our grandma and Pop Pop, we would go to Barnegat Bay to go crabbing and then Pop Pop cooked them up. After dinner, my aunt washed the dishes while the kids dried. The hard work flew as we sang songs and harmonized together, sounding pretty good. When the last dish had been tucked into the cupboard, the entire extended family took a walk on the boardwalk. The voices from those who meant the most to me wafted over and around me, surrounding me with a soft layer of comfort and safety. The adults talked while the kids ran and whooped and hollered and skipped. Sometimes a game of tag broke out until we got a little too rambunctious. Back at the beach house, the kids, exhausted, fell asleep in sleeping bags on the screened-in patio while the adults played cards.

When we weren't at the Jersey shore, we were at Aunt June's (Mom's best friend from high school), hanging out in her pool. It was there that I had my first tangible experience with the idea that God might think about me as an individual, and be concerned about my well-being.

I was in the backyard by myself, playing in the pool. I usually stayed in the shallow end, especially when no one was present as I didn't know how to swim very well. I played bobbing games, and holding my breath games. I held onto the side and kicked, seeing how high the water would splash. Then I moved my fingers along the pocked cement rim of the pool, scooting along like a little crab around the inside lip. I planned to go around the entire pool like this, but for some reason, my fingers slipped and I lost my grip. As I sank into the water, I couldn't get my footing on the bottom because it was like a slick river stone, coated with moss. The more I tried to run up the incline toward the shallow end, the farther I fell back. I didn't want to panic, but I knew no one was around. How much longer could I hold my breath?

And then, someone pulled me up until I was holding onto the edge of the pool again. I looked around to see who had helped me, but no one was there. I certainly hadn't done that on my strength. I didn't understand what had happened, but one thing I believed for certain: God had intervened to save me. It's cliché to say that I knew God saved me for some special purpose, but I don't know of any other way to put it. God seemed to have a future plan for me, because dying that day wasn't part of it.

In the winter, we Bausmiths were still tromping around outside. The pond by the elementary school would freeze over. We'd lace up our skates and race and make circles on the bumpy ice, nose hairs frozen, rosy cheeks responding to the cold, little clouds of breath hanging in the air. A perfect sledding hill nearby gave us a slick, shriek-filled ride down. We'd tumble into piles of snow at the bottom, laughing and starting impromptu snowball fights. We loved to make snowmen, complete with the requisite stick arms, and odd objects for eyes and buttons.

When I was twelve years old, my father got a job in California and moved my family from New Jersey to the West Coast. We traded snow for year-round beach, and were not sorry we did.

In high school, I wanted to be involved in so many things—like cheerleading, drill squad, or the gymnastics team—but would find myself chickening out. On my own, without Dad and Joanne by my side, I had a low confidence level and was nervous to try new things. I don't know why drama was different, but I enjoyed acting and had a number of roles in school plays.

Like most teenagers, as fun as high school could be, I counted the days until graduation when I could set my sights on moving to an apartment. I dreamed of owning a business, being my own boss, and having a staff underneath my care. I didn't expect it to happen right away, and wasn't sure of what steps I needed to take to get there. I wasn't even sure of what kind of business I wanted to own. I just knew that this goal called to me often from my daydreams.

I also dreamed of Africa, picturing myself in an African village, surrounded with village woman and children, communicating through love and teaching. I saw myself teaching them something—maybe crocheting, or sewing, or some kind of craft. Something they could make that would be useful.

After graduation, I took a job at a convalescent home, where I worked as a nurse's aid. I enjoyed helping people and taking care of them. I thought about becoming a nurse, but didn't know if I'd last through the years of schooling it would take to get that kind of education. If I went back to school, I'd have to continue living with my parents. I didn't know if I could do that! My whole being yearned for independence. I longed to take responsibility for my life, get a car, and have my own apartment. A friend and I attempted the latter the summer after we graduated, but no landlord would rent to us. I supposed we looked too young. Instead, we were resigned to do what we both dreaded—stay at home and rent from our parents.

I felt trapped, and began to look for my way out.

chapter 3

Escape Route

The hot sand shifted beneath my feet. Joanne and I lifted our beach towels, letting the soft breeze flutter them as we lowered them to the sand. I raised my hand as a visor over my eyes.

"Do you see those cute guys?" Joanne asked.

I smiled. "Yes."

It was not by accident that we had planted ourselves so close to the group of guys who looked quite promising.

Our friends set up their blanket next to our towels and perched the radio on one corner and tuned it to 99.7. All the hits, all the time.

Joanne and I spent as much time at Coral Beach as we could. I loved the sound of the crashing ocean, the tangy salt air, eating the fresh-from-the-fryer tortilla strips that we dipped into delicious salsa, and ice cream perched on waffle cones purchased from the weather-worn wood shacks that lined the shore. I loved reading a great novel while soaking up the sun's rays. The only thing I didn't like was parading about in my bathing suit. I felt so *fat*. That morning I'd put on my suit at least ten times, removing it and putting it back on. Should I go and inflict my obese body on everyone? No! Yes! No! The lure of the beach finally won. I groaned as I put the suit on for the last time and caught my reflection in the mirror. I turned away before the sight could change my mind again. I threw a sundress on to cover most of the depressing bulk.

In spite of my embarrassment at being seen in what I perceived to be my fat body, I would rather be at the beach than anywhere else.

Joanne stretched out next to me with her novel. I closed my eyes, sensing each of the sun's rays soaking warmth into every cell. After baking a little while, I sat up to survey the landscape. The cutest guy with the nearby group stood staring at the water, as if contemplating whether or not to go down to it. I decided to give him every reason to make that decision. I stood, brushing the sand off my backside and walked slowly by their encampment. I stopped at the edge of the ocean, letting the foamy water nibble at my toes. I sighed and hoped he would want to come strike up a conversation with me. I forced myself to keep looking out at the vast horizon, sort of watching some guy who flopped around in the water as if making an attempt at something a little bit like swimming.

Then, a male's teasing-toned voice sounded behind me. "That guy looks like he's ready to swim the English Channel, don't ya think?"

I laughed and turned. But this wasn't the boy I'd had my eye on! This one was shorter, had curly, brown hair, and a mischievous look in his hazel eyes. He sported orange trunks with a big, ol' safety pin holding them up. I put my hand up to my mouth to hide my grin—or to hold back laughing at those trunks. In a flash, I somehow knew he wouldn't mind.

He introduced himself as Robert, a junior high school math teacher in the San Fernando Valley. As we chatted, I realized several things almost immediately—Robert was fun; Robert was playful; Robert was *an older man*! I tried to ask sly questions to give me an idea as to how much older he was. I couldn't pin it down for certain, but I knew he must be at least seven years older than I. *Wow.*

We stood there with the water curling around our ankles, chatting about things I couldn't possibly remember. I do know I liked him a lot. In his straightforward manner, he revealed he liked me as well. "How about going sailing with me next weekend? I have a little sunfish."

My mind spun with the possibility. Did he mean he wanted the date to last the *whole weekend? Wouldn't that mean overnight?* Without skipping a beat, I blurted, "That sounds like fun, but you'll have to come over and meet my father."

Inside I cringed at what I'd said. I wasn't sure how I felt about an overnight date, much less an overnight being the *first* date. I hadn't messed around with boys, so this idea weakened my knees. I *was* certain that my little suggestion would cancel the invitation.

Robert smiled. "Of course. I would like to meet your father."

I tried to act all of my grown-up eighteen years so he wouldn't think I was a stupid little girl. "I'm glad," I said.

"ROBERT!" came a call from up the beach. "WE'RE GOING. COME ON."

Robert looked at me. "Can I have your number?"

"Sure. Do you have a pen?"

"Do I look like I could be hiding something to write with?" he teased.

"I don't have one either." I felt a bit of sadness, knowing I wouldn't see this good-looking boy, I mean, *man*, again.

"That's okay," he said. "I'm a math teacher. I like numbers. Go ahead; I'll remember."

I told him, believing with all my heart that either he'd forget, or he was just trying to be nice.

He repeated the number, then ran up the beach after his friends. I watched his friends and him climb the hill and surround a beautiful white Mustang convertible. Robert hopped over the driver's door and slipped in behind the wheel.

Wow. I really hoped he'd remember my number now. I couldn't wait to ride and be seen in that hot machine!

I spent the rest of the afternoon daydreaming about Robert, rehashing every word of our conversation. At the end of the day I went home ... to wait.

Once home, I knew he wouldn't call. There was no way he'd remember my number. I tried, but didn't succeed in putting him out of my head. I replayed every moment over and over, sometimes to try to squeeze out anything I might have missed from his words or body language, and sometimes just to enjoy those moments as if they were happening for the first time.

About three days later, the ringing phone was for me. "Hi, Barbara! This is Robert. We met at the beach on Saturday."

I paused, trying to play it cool. "Oh, yes, I remember."

Barbara and Robert "before kids."

"I was hoping I could meet your father so we could go out to dinner next Saturday. Would that work out?"

Would it! I didn't even bring up the sailing idea, kind of glad he forgot, but so glad he remembered the most important thing—my phone number. "I think so. I'll see when my dad can meet you."

Dad agreed to meet him immediately before our date. That day I stressed about what to wear. I settled on a sundress with a smocked bodice with daisies embroidered into it. I curled my hair, put on mascara, baby-blue eye shadow and a slightly pearlescent lip color. When the doorbell rang, I wanted to fling open the door, but instead opened it with as much calm as I could muster. Robert and I exchanged big smiles. "Hi," I said.

"I'm looking for Barbara," he said, still smiling.

"I'm Barbara."

Robert looked so surprised. "Really? I guess you look different with wet hair and in a bathing suit. I didn't recognize you with your clothes on." He grinned even bigger, later telling me that he was delighted that the girl he'd asked out was even better looking dry and clothed.

I invited Robert inside, and we sat in the living room with my mother and father. My dad asked the usual questions, "How old are you?" "What do you do?"

Robert answered directly, without looking away. I knew my dad would be impressed with that.

After a little more chit chat, my father said, "Make sure you have my daughter home before 10:00."

I couldn't believe it! I felt like a baby. "Dad," I tried to say respectfully, "would it be all right if we stayed out a little longer? Like until 11:00?"

He looked at me, then Robert. "All right," he said.

Then I knew my mother had talked with him earlier and softened my father a bit before meeting Robert.

After getting Dad's approval, Robert ushered me out to … a white VW Bug.

"Where's the Mustang?" I blurted.

He flashed me that grin again. "It's my cousin's. On our way up the hill, I asked him if we could pretend it was my car."

I wanted to slug him, but he was too cute, too adorably funny. And really, it didn't matter what he drove.

He took me to a Mexican restaurant in Santa Monica where we talked and laughed, and ended the date by walking along the beach. Afterward, Robert drove me home and walked me to the door, not even trying to kiss me. I liked that a lot. I felt he respected me and didn't want to push too fast.

I wish I could say that from that moment, we were an item. But Robert had ties to another girl I didn't know about. When he continued to not kiss me goodnight, I got suspicious. I eventually caught him on a date with another girl.

If I'm going to date you," I told him the next day, "then I'm going to be the only one dating you." I wasn't about to share my guy with anyone. And if he wanted to share, why, he could just take a hike off the Santa Monica pier.

He looked a little surprised, but he said, "Well, okay."

I think he'd already been on the way to making that decision for himself. And soon afterwards, he kissed me—with a kiss so amazing, I couldn't believe how fortunate I was to be dating him. I was hooked!

Most of our dates were eating out, going to movies, or just hanging out. I would go over to his house on weekends and help him with whatever he was doing—usually working on a car. We'd go to the trash dump to find parts and items he could use for his many projects. I'd keep him company while he worked on the VW Bug. I didn't care what we did. I just loved being with him.

On the anniversary of our seven months of dating, we were in Mom's kitchen fixing lunch. Robert, being his usual silly self, cornered me. "Give me a kiss, darlin'," he said, sounding a bit like a Southern hillbilly—if there was such a thing.

"No," I giggled. "Mom might come in and catch us."

"All the better," he said, waggling his eyebrows at me. "Live dangerously!" He moved in to kiss me and I pulled back and touched my fingers to his mouth.

"No," I said again, only serious this time. "If you love me, and want to be with me, then what are we waiting for? I think we should get married."

He laughed nervously and said, "Whoa, whoa, whoa, wait a minute. Aren't we going kinda fast here? I don't know whether I'm ready to get married or not."

I knew he wanted to get married to someone fairly soon. He'd said as much over the months. He had waited to date seriously until he had a good teaching job. Now that he had one, and I was here and in love with him, I thought it was time to take that step.

From my perspective, I wanted to marry him because he was loving and made me feel special. I loved the strength he exuded. I loved that fact that he was so sure in his opinions and could voice them. Add to that his great job, and I knew he would always be able to provide for our family.

I looked at him. "Well, I am ready, and if you want to be with me, then we need to start making plans to get married."

I suppose I startled Robert, and it was one of the few times in our lives when I would be the obvious decision-maker. But he didn't hesitate to give me his answer. "Okay."

At first Robert was concerned that I only wanted to marry him to get away from my father. Granted, Dad still put a curfew on me, and made me adhere to a bunch of other house rules. And maybe Robert was a little bit right. But I believed he was my soulmate and that God had brought us together.

For a dreamy-eyed young girl like me, Robert was the fulfillment of all my dreams. Together we would be *one*, as I'd heard mentioned many times in my past. Together we would play and laugh and have babies. When he was not at work, we would spend every waking hour together. From now on, my life would be complete. I could hardly wait.

Over the next five months, my mother helped me plan the wedding that would bring those dreams in for a landing. I didn't care much for the specifics of the wedding, leaving those to my distressed mother who couldn't understand a young bride not caring about the details.

Mother worked for the May Company department store. So, Robert and I took full advantage of her 20 percent discount on all merchandise, buying our wedding rings and my wedding dress with it. I didn't have much of a sense of style, and I didn't really care. I did, however, find it very important to have *something old, something new, something borrowed, something blue.* For something old, I planned to carry my mother's small, white prayer book that she had carried in her wedding. My dress and shoes were new. I borrowed a Spanish mantilla veil (which didn't match the style of my dress at all), and wore a blue garter, edged with lace, high on my thigh. Since no wedding could be perfect, I had a giant zit on my face—which showed up quite nicely in the wedding photos. But I didn't think anyone could tell I also wore a fall to augment my very short hair, and Lee press-on nails to augment my very short nails.

My sisters and best friend served as my attendants and carried bouquets of flowers attached to purple fans—an attempt to tie in my very Spanish veil with their very non-Spanish outfits.

Promises of the life I'd always dreamed about thrived in my heart when, on June 22, 1969, I became Mrs. Robert Cameron. I was more than ready to dive into adult life head on—now officially on my own— making my own rules and living my life the way I wanted to. I had never been so excited, or more filled with emotion, as the day Robert and I exchanged our vows. My life, a perfectly budding flower, was ready to open into full bloom.

More than anything else, on that day, I not only vowed it, but I knew beyond the shadow of a doubt—I would never look at another man.

chapter 4

The Family Nest

Robert and I began our married life as most couples do: filled
with hopes, dreams, and expectations. We took ours with us on a
honeymoon at Lake Mead in Nevada. We camped for a few days
before our invited friends came to join us to water ski, boat, and
generally have a complete blast. That is, until I fried in the sun and
had to hide out in a motel for the rest of the planned days away.
Robert's brother and my sister Joanne took new notice of each other,
and we could see the interchange of chemistry and sparks between
them.

As a typical, poor, young married couple, our finances were
extremely tight. I didn't mind where we lived or how slim our budget.
I swam in the sea of love, basking in the joy of being married. Some
of Robert's harshness brought me up short, and I held back the many
tears. Certain he didn't mean it, I forgave quickly, and moved on.

I've often felt that I've basically had an easy life. Things I didn't
deserve landed in my lap over and over. I don't know why this would
happen to me, but it did. And so, when Robert's parents left the
country after our wedding, needing house-sitters for a year, it was
another undeserved gift, which we eagerly and gratefully accepted.

Robert and I didn't talk much about when we'd have babies or
how many, but it didn't really matter, for shortly after we were
married, we found out that baby number one would soon be on the
way. Although I hadn't expected to be a mom so soon, I looked

forward to cuddling that sweet one in my arms. I made myself busy redesigning Robert's former bedroom into a nursery for our little one. I would talk to God as I went, as if He were sitting in the rocking chair in the corner, watching me decorate. "Dear Lord," I'd say, "I pray that this baby will be healthy. I pray that I will be a good mom. Thank you for giving me this gift of being a mom."

Like most parents, we went through lists and books, trying to decide on a name. Robert, a total Trekkie, said that if it was a boy, he wanted to name him Kirk after Captain Kirk of the *Starship Enterprise*. Even though I wasn't sure about naming my kid after a character in a TV series, I did like the name Kirk. I looked it up in the baby-name dictionary to see what it meant. When I saw that Kirk meant "of the church," a knowing split through me, and I knew it was perfect! That's what I wanted to name him!

Kirk was born on October 12, 1970, after a very easy delivery. We *oohed* and *aahed* over him, my heart bursting with love and joy as I'd never known. This little boy stole our hearts from the first day. We couldn't get enough of him. Robert scooped him up the minute he got home from work, and made funny noises to make him laugh.

When Robert's folks returned home from their extended trip, we packed up what little we had and moved in with Robert's brother, who would eventually marry my sister Joanne.

I didn't think I could get pregnant right away after having Kirk. I soon discovered the combination of ignorance and an irresistible husband creates another baby right away.

Robert wanted to continue to endow his kids with crew member names from the *Starship Enterprise* and proposed we name the next child *Spock*!

"Are you out of your mind?"

"Don't you think that would be cool?" Robert asked, that gleam I knew too well in his eyes.

"Are you serious?" I said. "No, I don't think so."

"Please?" he said, giving me that cute look he knew I couldn't resist.

But this time I did resist. "NO." I smiled at him and climbed onto his lap. "If it's a girl, I want her name to start with the letter B just like mine ..."

Robert shrugged. "I still think Spock ..."

I ignored him and continued, "… and give her the middle name, Jeanne, after my mother." I leaned over and engaged him in a very convincing kiss.

Eleven months after Kirk was born, his sister, Bridgette Jeanne, made her appearance on September 14, 1971. We couldn't believe our fortune to have two darling babies to fill our hearts with love.

We couldn't keep living with family, and we didn't have enough money to buy a house. So we moved to an apartment in Canoga Park, which would be close to Robert's work. I wasn't there five minutes before my neighbor across the hall burst out to introduce herself. "Hi, I'm Fran Rich. If you need anything, just let me know." She gave me a brilliant, inviting smile, making it clear she meant it. Fran and I became friends.

In a moment, in the blink of an eye, things happen that you have no idea carry any importance at all. Meeting Fran was one of those life-altering encounters that I wouldn't understand for years to come.

Our lives in the apartment were uneventful, really. Just the normal daily lives of a young married couple with two small kids trying to make ends meet. Because it seemed we'd never be able to get on our feet, Robert's parents loaned us the money to make a down payment on a new house in Fillmore that hadn't been built yet. We drove out to the building site a lot, dreaming, planning, being excited. I cherished those moments, because it seemed more and more like Robert and I really had two separate lives. It didn't seem like we spent much time together anymore. At least going to view our new house gave us time together to think about the same things.

My heart longed for him. Every afternoon I'd wait with the babies on the front stoop, eager for him to come home. He'd pull up in the VW Bug and hop out. Maria, the buxom, Hispanic neighbor who lived on the floor above us, would wave and say in her squeaky, childlike voice, "Hello, Robert."

Robert would give me a cursory, "Hello, honey," then run past, eager to have a little gab fest with Maria.

A bomb of inadequacy went off in my heart, and I sat there, trying to be stoic and pick up the pieces.

I knew attractive women drew Robert to them like a kid to an ice cream truck, and so I did all I could to dress in a way I knew would please him. I fought the continual weight battle, made more difficult

with two babies in quick succession. Before he got home I'd change, brush my hair, and spray on a little perfume. But it didn't seem to matter. He seemed to need Maria's affirmation as much as I needed his.

Every time he bounded up those stairs, eager to see Maria, my own insecurity dug a deeper pit for me to fall in, jealousy built a bigger room, and self-consciousness dressed me in its funky wardrobe.

I adored my husband in spite of the way he looked at beautiful women and talked with them. I don't suppose it helped when I put on a show of an understanding wife by laughing and joking as if his appreciation of attractive, buxom women didn't bother me. Instead, I kept my slow dying on the inside, where no one could see.

As successful as I was at putting on a mask in one area, I didn't succeed in others. We seemed to fight a lot until I would just clam up and back off, letting Robert have what he wanted. It seemed easier that way. And it stopped his lashing words from slicing more wounds into my heart.

When we married, I hadn't realized that Robert had made a private vow: that no woman would ever control him. His mother was the commanding force in the family. It was tough growing up in a home where the woman made most of the decisions. Robert had a difficult time with his mother and he had trouble respecting his father for not being a stronger father figure. Robert's vow was so strong that he saw many things as control, even when they were not. A woman having a different opinion felt like control. A woman having a personal desire felt like control. And Robert's only method of dealing with the perceived control was to beat it back with harsh words. As long as I didn't do anything that seemed like control to him, he could be funny, sweet, and charming. But step one toe over that invisible boundary, and *whammo*! I got it good.

Robert never, ever hit me. But his words landed hard on my heart. Sometimes he joked with others, and his words were funny, but they were insensitive to me, and hurt my feelings. I tried to talk to him about it, but it always ended up in such a tangled mess that my simple mind couldn't come up with words or ideas fast enough to counteract what he was saying. So I let it go. I had my babies. I had a husband who worked hard to provide for us. I still wished we could be *one* like I'd heard somewhere that couples were supposed to be. But that dream was slipping away—fast.

One day, Fran and I sat on the front stoop of our apartment building, basking in the sun and watching our children race tricycles and big wheels up and down the sidewalk. Her light brown-haired, five-year-old son, Adam, was exactly two years older than my tow-head, Kirk. Both sported fashionable bowl haircuts. Both could strap on an impish grin and captivate females in a heartbeat. Both giggled as though a fountain of laughter continually bubbled up from an unending spring within them. My wispy-haired Bridgette waved her chubby toddler hands and clapped in delight whenever the boys rumbled past. She bobbed in a little dance, sometimes attempting a twirl, but landing flat on her diapered bottom, only to chortle at the vibrating thump it made throughout her tiny body.

Fran ran her fingers through her close-cropped dark hair. "Barbara," she said, her voice thick with her New York Jewish upbringing. "I really think you oughta get your kids into the business.

Candace, Melissa, Bridgette and Kirk ham it up.

They're cute. I told ya. I'll introduce you to Adam's agent. I bet she could get them on commercials, too."

I shook my head. "Thanks, Fran. But I don't think so." I enjoyed being a mom. I liked spending time with my kids. I rubbed my yet unnamed and unknown newest addition due to arrive sometime in October. I didn't see how being on commercials would be anything but more stuff to do when life was already full with my family and the home Robert and I were soon moving to in Fillmore.

Fran's brown eyes looked from me to her son. Delight and a bit of awe started in her eyes, moved to her mouth, and then lifted her hands into motion. "Just look at him! Isn't he darling?" She rested her elbows on her knees, chin on her hands, watching her commercial actor zip around a pole and pedal furious feet around and around. "I think you're nuts not to try it."

I smiled. Sure, Adam was cute. It was fun to see him on TV from time to time. But my kids? No way. Who would want them on television? They were just my kids. Darling to their father and me, our greatest joy (and sometimes our greatest frustration). Basic, blond, American kids; a dime a dozen. Nothing special. Kirk was shy, but ready with that easy laugh. Bridgette was talkative and outgoing, eager

to be everyone's friend — even as a toddler. Traipsing around
Hollywood, battling other parents for a spot in the limelight was not
my idea of fun. Besides, I knew there was hardly a reason my kids
would have a chance against a thousand others. All I wanted was to
love them, take good care of them, discipline them, and make sure
they had everything they needed to be happy.

Fran continued to suggest I take the kids to her agent. She didn't
nag, but she was persistent. I always smiled and said the same thing.

After eighteen months in the apartment, our home in Fillmore
was completed. It was tough to say good-bye to Fran. We'd become
good friends and confidantes. Kirk and Adam got along well together.
I enjoyed having a neighbor so close that we could pop into each
other's apartments for that missing egg, a moment of venting about
being a mom, or sharing our latest shopping spree. But I also looked
forward to having our own home nestled in the hills of Fillmore,
California. On moving day, Fran and I hugged, tears in our eyes.
"Keep in touch, 'kay?" I said.

"Of course," Fran said, letting her hands slide to my wrists. "I'll
miss ya, Barb."

I turned away, not able to really think that this was good-bye. I
planned to keep her in my heart, even if we couldn't see each other
much.

I cherished our brand-new home. It was a beautiful two-story in
a cul-de-sac — the only two-story house on the block. We felt like the
kings of the cul-de-sac.

We made friends with our neighbors, who all went together and
pitched in to pour sidewalks, to make brick walls and patios, and to
landscape. I even shoveled sand to help mix the cement and would
trowel the brick seams. Robert appreciated it all and learned a lot.

Our time in Fillmore flew by as we added brown-eyed Melissa
Rachelle on October 3, 1974, and then blue-eyed Candace Helaine
on April 6, 1976. Both girls were darlings, who we welcomed with as
much joy as the first two.

Robert supplemented his income as a math teacher by purchasing
fixer-upper homes and by refurbishing old VW Bugs. Our family
would move into the homes and live there until Robert finished
making his repairs. Once he did, he'd find another, and we'd move
on. It was kind of fun for a while, but after Candace arrived, I decided

I wanted to settle into one home and neighborhood where we could raise our family. Robert had found a tract home in a quiet neighborhood in Canoga Park—the same town where we'd lived in the apartment across from Fran. We moved in when Kirk was eight and never left.

I had hoped that once we had our family, Robert would agree to go to church. When I first married, I'd been glad to be a little rebellious and not go to church. It wasn't that I was intentionally rebelling against *God*, just going to *church*. I wanted the chance to make my own grown-up, adult decisions apart from my parents. They had taken me to church my entire growing-up years, and I was tired of it. I knew all the appropriate information. God was almighty and holy and to be completely revered and feared. Jesus died for our sins. You ask Jesus into your heart to be saved (whatever that meant). What more was there to being a Christian than that?

As my family had blossomed into completeness, I wanted to take them to church. I missed it. And I was hoping that if we went to church, Robert would follow along. When we married, I'd never even thought to ask if he believed in God. I just presumed he did and that all would be well.

When I asked Robert if we could all go to church, his answer, was, "NO."

"Why?" I asked, feeling myself shrink inside my skin.

"I don't believe in God. Besides, I'd rather be doing something else on Sundays. Something fun."

"It wouldn't hurt for the kids to go to Sunday school, would it?"

"I want us to be together as a family. When the kids are older, they can choose what they want to believe. It's not right for parents to tell them what they should and should not believe. That's their choice. Their decision."

I looked up to Robert. Seven years older, college-educated, a *teacher*. He knew far more than I, an uneducated girl who got married immediately out of high school. I trusted him. His reason sounded good and right. Reluctantly, I agreed.

So, instead of going to church on Sundays, we established the tradition of taking the kids to the beach with our family friends, the Rocks.

Robert and Rusty Rock had grown up together, near neighbors and attending the same elementary school. Rusty met Patty while they were both involved in gymnastics at the local college. Patty joined the friendship Robert and Rusty had established, and all three added me to the mix when I came along years later.

Rusty and Patty had the unique job of being circus performers—high-wire trapeze artists who performed all over the country. When they weren't traveling, Rusty put his hand to finish carpentry and was marvelous at it. They often bunked with us when they were in town. Our kids loved their boys, Andrew and Ryan, and the six of them got along well. They played, rough-housed, rode bikes and scooters in the backyard while the adults hashed over the more important issues of life—issues that usually involved Robert making us laugh.

Rusty Rock and Barbara on one of the family "beach days" ... with Barb on the bottom.

After dinner, we'd send the kids off to bed with the theme song from the Roy Rogers' show. "Happy trails to you," the adults bellowed as the kids groaned and complained.

Patty and Rusty appreciated ice cream as much as we did, and we often polished off a half-gallon of Rocky Road after the kids were supposed to be in bed. The kids caught on, though, and yelled, "That's not fair!"

When Robert said he wanted to do something fun on Sundays, he meant it. Every warm Sunday for years, our family and the Rocks went to Santa Monica beach together. My kids had both the Bausmith and Cameron blood in them—taking to being on, in, or near the water every chance we got. Robert's father, George, a gymnast and beach lover, had done routines at Muscle Beach during his youth, teaching his kids to love both as well. I think this is why we went so much.

On beach Sundays we did gymnastics, learning from the Rocks, and applying what we'd learned from Robert's father. The kids learned how to do balancing tricks. The kids body-surfed, skim-boarded, dug holes, and built sand castles. The little ones rolled around in the sand and dug for sand crabs. The tradition of body surfing became quite an event where the guys would have competitions. Whoever landed farthest up on the sand, won. The dads would cheat, using their fingers to crawl along the bottom when the water didn't take them far enough.

Patty and I kept our eyes out for the youngest ones when they were little, then happily moved on to munching Wheat Thins and reading romance novels when they were old enough to not run off or drown if we took our eyes off them for an instant.

On the way home, Robert stopped at Foster's Freeze to get frosty cones for all the kids.

Those were the best days. It didn't matter that sand made our peanut butter and jelly sandwiches crunchy. Or that I felt so fat, I hid behind a blanket when someone wanted to take a picture. Or that at the end of the day we were all exhausted. Our happiest family memories are based on Sundays at the beach.

Robert loved his kids. But he didn't really know what to do with Kirk. I encouraged him to let Kirk help him build or work on a car, but Robert always said, "I need to get it done. I'll get it done faster on my own." And so Kirk and his father never really connected or got close as I hoped father and son would. Respect thrived, but not affection.

However, the girls remember their father as being affectionate and funny. He hugged on them, kissed them, and wanted to play.

Candace : He was fun. When he wasn't angry, he was a funny guy. He had a great, dry sense of humor, and he loved to kid.

Melissa : We did a lot of fun, physical things with him. Fun activity things with him.

Bridgette : We'd come to the table and say, "What's for dessert?" and Dad would say, "Desert the table."

Robert and I encouraged the kids musically. We sang around the house—I especially loved to sing or play my music really loud while cleaning. Robert played the trumpet, Bridgette danced, Melissa played the flute and a little bit of piano, while Kirk and Candace played only the piano. On our many car trips, we listened for hours to cassettes of old classics like "The Man on the Flying Trapeze," "It's My Job, and I Like It Fine," and "She'll Be Comin' Round the Mountain." We'd sing at the top of our lungs, not caring what people in the other cars thought.

Robert even hoped to make a music room out of the garage behind our house one day. Until then, he practiced his trumpet in the backyard.

Candace : I took piano lessons and my dad would sit at the piano every day with me and take me to all my lessons. He would get a little annoying with his knitting needle. He would be the metronome and tap the knitting needle on the piano.

Robert also loved teasing the kids and making them cringe and laugh at the same time. He had this horrific-looking red VW truck that he used to drive the kids to school. They were mortified to be seen in this mini-monstrosity. So they tried to be clever about getting their dad to drop them off far enough away from the school so no one would see them. "Hey, Dad," they'd say casually. "Why don't you just drop us off right here on this corner." He'd oblige, but then he'd drive around the block, returning at the precise moment they hit the school's front walk. He'd hang out the window and shout, "Hey, son, have a good day at school!" When he'd pick them up, he'd honk the horn to draw unnecessary attention to the beast of a car.

Robert and I both believed in disciplining the kids. We grew up in homes where discipline was administered; we were taught that there were consequences for disobeying the rules.

Melissa : We had strict, strict parents.

Kirk : We always had to be in when the street lights went on.

Melissa : We always had a curfew. They always called when we were at someone else's house to be sure the parents were there. We were never allowed to be alone.

We liked to take the kids out to eat once in a while as a treat and to teach them public manners. In the car, Robert or I would say, "We're going out to dinner. Be on your best behavior, use your 'please' and 'thank-yous.' You are to sit at the table and not run around. If you misbehave, we aren't going out to dinner next week."

We received many compliments from people in the restaurants that our children were so well-behaved. After the folks gave their compliments and left, we'd turn to the children and tell them, "We're very proud of you. Someone gave you a compliment." And we were very proud of them. They were very well-mannered kids.

Candace : Once someone gave that compliment, it was like, "Whoo hoo! We're goin' out next Friday." It became a contest, who would remember to say, "Thank you" first to Mom and Dad for taking us out. I don't think it ever happened, but we knew the threat was there that if we didn't behave, they would get up and we would all have to leave. All of us were too scared to misbehave. Yeah, the wrath of Dad … So, they definitely taught us that kind of manners well.

I think that some of our discipline came from anger and frustration. I don't think I really knew how to explain to the kids that they had not only disappointed me and their father, but also God. And so instead of carefully administering well thought-out consequences, I just did what felt like the right thing at the moment. My kids tease that I often used the *clap-clap* to get their attention, or to highlight what I wanted them to do.

Robert could get very angry and yell at the kids, which scared them, or he could get in a goofy mood and turn things all around with one child and the rest of us weren't any the wiser.

We had agreed that when the kids were little and disobeyed, they would be spanked. Robert marched the disobedient children into a bedroom and would either spank or talk to them. One time Kirk knew his actions would land him a spanking, so he thought he'd fool his dad, and stuffed a book down the back of his pants before his dad got into the room. At first, Robert pointed out the book, trying not to laugh. "What is *that*?"

Kirk just looked up at his father, even more afraid than before.

"Lean over the bed."

Kirk leaned over.

"Now yell when I spank you."

Kirk looked at his father, wondering what in the world was going on, but with the first spank, let out a yell. He caught on, and continued to yell every time his father whacked the book.

One day, Robert marched Candace into her bedroom for a spanking. But the look in her eyes melted him. So he whispered, "Let's see how good of an actress you are. When I slap the belt across the bed, you scream and cry. Let's see if we can fool the other kids into thinking you were really getting spanked."

They enjoyed their little private joke so much that this went on for years. I never knew the two of them were coconspirators. Little did I know Candace was honing her acting skills while Robert was "disciplining" her.

Our family treasured being together, whatever we chose to do. Sometimes that cohesiveness worked well, and sometimes, it could work against the parents.

Robert hired a contractor to refurbish our kitchen, with Robert doing some of the work. Robert and the contractor had a disagreement, and the contractor refused to finish the work he had been hired to do. Robert decided that, as a family, we would make signs and picket the man's business. So we did, taking the kids with us, walking in circles in front of the business, and waving our signs. The job was done in three days.

Kirk took note of this, and when his father did something the kids were upset about, the kids found scrap lumber in the garage, and wrote signs on notebook paper with bubble letters.

Dad is a mean lean screaming machine!
Dad's on the Warpath!
Unfair Fathers!
Dad is a big bummer!

When Robert drove home from work that night, he found all his kids and some neighbor kids as well, all marching in a circle in the center of our street, chanting their slogans. We laughed about that for days.

Kirk picked up a lot of things from his father: his sense of humor, his love of relating to people, and his sense of right and wrong. Robert, however, wasn't known for tact. For example, he made it clear that people who smoked were stupid and were going to die. This made such a deep impression on Kirk that we could be driving around and Kirk would get all squirrelly in the back seat. "Dad!" he'd shout, stabbing his finger at the window. "Look! That lady's smoking! You'd better tell her, Dad. Tell her she shouldn't do that!"

Kirk picked up his introversion from me. He didn't mind being around those he knew, and in situations where he understood what was going on, but was really uncomfortable with new circumstances and avoided them as much as he could. He disliked being in the limelight, preferring to hide in the shadows. When home, if we didn't have friends over, he preferred to stay in his room and enjoy the quiet or his music.

Bridgette was our easy-going girl. She had the bubbly, positive, outgoing personality. I think she picked up the best traits of both Robert and me. We knew that when Bridgie grew up, her home would be where everyone would gather and feel safe, where kids would come for Kool-Aid after school, and no one would leave feeling unloved. She enjoyed being in the limelight and performing. She didn't have a shy bone in her body.

Melissa was tender, sensitive, and very definitely her own person. She had the Bausmith syndrome of being able to feel things deeply, and to cry at the drop of a hat. Melissa could remember details and

Melissa pickets her father for being unfair.

every aspect of events that happened long before. She would be our historian, whether she intended to be or not. Melissa also had my propensity to hold onto a little extra weight. By life standards, she was a normal little girl. By Hollywood standards, she'd be labeled "chubby."

Candace and her daddy got along the best. She was Robert's "Little Princess"—a fact that didn't go unnoticed by her sisters. This special bond was created in part because Candace *always* got Robert's jokes. Robert knew he could make her laugh, and so this was something that Robert appreciated about her.

Candace had a strong sense of right and wrong—even if she didn't always listen to that quiet voice of morality. When she was very little, she would throw a temper tantrum, flinging herself on the floor and holding her breath—showing the trait of being strong-willed that never really left.

Candace also wanted to prove to me that she could do things just like I could, so she purposefully picked up some of my traits and talents. Unfortunately, one of the ones she picked up is that she loved to shop! She favored clothes—especially shoes. She has a weakness for shopping to this day.

Robert and I could butt heads on many things, but we were pretty much on the same page in how we chose to raise these kids we'd made together and who were so much like both of us. We encouraged after-school activities such as T-ball, soccer, tap, and ballet lessons. We wanted our kids to be well-rounded and happy. We wanted them to have experiences in life that were fun. If they didn't have an afternoon activity on a particular day, they came home and played with neighborhood friends, the Rock kids, or cousins and rode bikes and Big Wheels, and watched TV. There was nothing different about our family that would set us apart from any other. Nothing that said we should stand out and be counted. Nothing that said we were special. We were just the Camerons, a law-abiding, moral family.

The only difference that could be noted is that we did put a higher priority on the value of *family* than some. Family was everything for us. We frequently socialized with family—whether with the kids' grandparents, aunts, uncles, or cousins. They would come to our house; we would go there. My sister Joanne and Robert's brother had kids the same age as ours, and we did a lot of casual dinners together. Our kids spent more time with family than they did with friends. Their best friends were each other.

Our strongest goals guided us to want to circle our wagons close, guard our children and raise them well. Nothing more. If you were good, held fast to high moral values, and taught them to your children, whom you loved, there was nothing finer in life.

chapter 5

Fran Steps In

I loved being a mother, but I wasn't so sure sometimes about all the stuff that went along with being a stay-at-home mom. Like most moms, there were days when I loved it, and days when I, well, didn't. Once my kids were almost all in school, the yearning for more tugged at me, begging for attention.

Although Robert loved me the only way he knew how, my soul craved for something more to fill it. Something intangible that I had expected that a husband would fulfill, but mine didn't. I wanted to be valued and validated at home, but felt more like a semi-appreciated housewife—a woman married to her house, not to her husband.

I enjoyed sewing, sometimes making matching outfits for the girls and me. I liked to entertain and make fun foods, experimenting along the way. I liked raising my kids, spending time with them, instilling inside their precious little hearts the things that were important to me: Share, be kind to everyone, be polite, it's better to give than to receive, be respectful of others—especially their elders. Treat others as you would like them to treat you.

My dream of having my own business became a very small reality as I gave macramé lessons and home parties. After one, I was so excited, waving bills and shouting, "Robert! I made nineteen dollars!"

Opposite page: *The photo given to Fran Rich to present to Iris Burton.*
Left to right: *Bridgette, Kirk, Melissa, and cousin Jennifer.*

41

"Excellent, darlin'," Robert replied, impressed with my haul. "Let's go get ice cream."

And off we'd go, feeling rich with our small windfall.

The macramé was fun, and somewhat fulfilling, but still, I longed for so much more. I wanted to *be* someone. And being "just a mom" felt lonely and sad sometimes. I missed the man I married. He spent most of his free time practicing trumpet, tinkering with cars, or remodeling houses. He'd tell me I was doing a good job, but still, something huge was missing from our marriage.

Robert seemed to *like* me, but not *value* me. We'd go out to dinner at our favorite little Mexican hole-in-the-wall, Mission Burrito. It didn't cost much, so it was a good, cheap date. But while we ate, he might spend the entire time talking to someone at the table next to us, to the servers, or to a guest at our table. Robert amazed me at how well he could ask questions and keep people talking. He probed deeper and deeper, wanting to hear their story, wanting to know what made them tick.

I sat, silently eating my warm chicken salad and feeling stupid because I couldn't think of a thing to add or a question of my own to ask. I felt left out of the conversation. Certainly it didn't matter if I was even there. Sometimes I wondered when he'd ask me those kinds of questions again—as he did when we were first dating. Did he really think he knew me well enough to not need to ask those questions? Or wasn't he interested?

Any beautiful girl paying attention to him swept him off his feet. Oh, how he loved to have conversations with beautiful women. If they flirted, he flirted right back.

"How can you do that to me?" I asked him once.

"It's only a game, Barb. There's no harm in it. It's fun."

"But it hurts me."

"I'm *married* to you," he'd answer as if I didn't get it.

And I didn't. All I knew was that these encounters made me feel invisible—as though he didn't value me as a special, unique woman at all.

On the other hand, Robert had a great sense of humor. His wit created a trail of laughter wherever he went. He was so smart, his intelligence and quick mind obvious to all he met. He could make friends with anyone—and did. He had a high sense of moral value—even while not believing in God or any kind of moral, "higher power."

He loved to learn things and became quite good at whatever he set his mind to: carpentry, car mechanics, cement-pouring, and wall-making.

He had all these great qualities, yet coupled with how often he ignored me, said derogatory or insensitive things to me, and created a kind of confusing soup in my simple self. I looked up to him and respected him, but I felt like the puppy who alternately gets loved on and kicked—never knowing which is coming next. One minute he could have me laughing, the next wishing I could escape his insensitivity and cruelty.

I tried to be good—the best wife I could be, but I never seemed good enough.

But sometimes his incredible generous heart came through, reminding me that he was a good man somewhere deep inside.

Not too long after I'd given birth to Candace, Robert came home from work troubled about one of his kids in PE. "John's a nice kid, Barb. But he's fat. The kids are ripping him apart."

I hated hearing stories like that. It was so unfair.

"He wants to go to the prom to prove he's not a total loser. But he can't find a date anywhere." Robert looked at me. "I feel so bad for him."

Shortly afterwards, we ran across John, and I said, "Hey, John, if you can't find a date for the prom, I'll go with you."

"Would you really?" The kid's face lit up like a Hollywood marquee.

Snapshots of an unwanted kid being tortured by cruel classmates came to mind. "Of course I'll go!" I said, not really expecting him to take me up on it.

But he did—with Robert's approval. "I think it's great." Robert reached across the table and squeezed my hand. "You'll knock 'em dead."

John was beside himself with joy. He didn't want us to stay long— just long enough to make an appearance and get our pictures taken.

The night arrived. I had done my long, blond hair into curls— half up, half down. I wore a beautiful, long, yellow dress, and took care with my makeup. I had loved acting in high school, and even with the sudden migraine, this would be my most fun performance yet. I stepped out of the bedroom to model for Robert.

"Big John" and Barb at the prom. Barbara was 26 years old and had recently given birth to Candace.

"Darlin'! Look at you!" Robert crooned. "You look like a beauty queen."

I blushed, warming with his rare praise.

John arrived in a Rolls-Royce, presented me with a rose corsage, and escorted me to the car. We arrived at the prom venue a little late on purpose, so the full effect of his "date" wouldn't be lost on his peers. When he showed up with a blonde on his arm, his classmates couldn't believe it. For a moment, everything stopped. Then questions shot about the room, whispers hissing as we walked by, me on his arm. "Who is she?"

John had said he was bringing a date who didn't attend that school, but lived up north. No one believed him, and no one believed he would bring anything but a girl who looked like a stray dog. We had our pictures taken, danced a few dances, smiled a lot at a sea of curious faces, then left.

John thanked me profusely, but it had totally been my pleasure. Anything I could do to encourage an underdog, to love the unlovable, to bring into value those who felt undervalued was incredibly important to me. It brought me tremendous satisfaction and great joy to elevate them to the status everyone deserves—being people equal to others, no one better than anyone else. That night at the prom, John changed from disrespected, dorky, fat kid to a bit of a mystery. I still laugh, wondering what those kids thought about during and after the prom. "Hey, man, he must have something we missed."

Robert and I loved opening our hearts and home to others. It gave me a chance to pour into others the qualities I found so important in my life: caring, compassion, and empathy. Robert, the eternal extrovert, needed insatiable amounts of people-contact to keep his energy flying high. I, being the introvert, liked the others carrying the evening. Secretly, I was also glad for the people to distract us from our own marriage issues, giving us something tangible and outside ourselves to focus on.

For some reason, people came to us with their problems. Perhaps it was because of Robert's ability to ask questions that made their issues become clear. Or—the teacher coming out in him—his flip charts on easels with pointer sticks. Maybe it was how we loved to listen and encourage others. Or maybe it was just my chocolate chip

Bridgette and Melissa performing with their Donny and Marie microphones.

cookies. My kids say our time with these hurting people impacted them. They noticed how others respected us, and seeing that built a greater sense of awe and respect for us.

I wanted to have the hurting people come because I hoped they would find compassion and peace in my home. I listened to them pouring out their hearts and hoped that somehow we helped. It was odd, though, that we couldn't help ourselves.

We also wanted to just plain have fun. Adults, kids, we didn't care. Come one, come all—an open-house attitude that almost invited danger years later when Kirk was at the height of stardom.

One attraction that brought kids to our house was a 1948 Rock-Ola bubbler jukebox that Robert refurbished. He took old 45 rpm record singles, and glued them back-to-back, so we could double our "hit" song list. He stocked the jukebox with true oldies, then added a few of the kids' favorite artists including Prince, Duran-Duran, and Sheila E.

The kids enjoyed punching in the numbers to their favorite songs and dancing. Enticing their friends to come over wasn't a problem with the Rock-Ola. It was cool, a novelty, and a source of hours of endless fun for the entire neighborhood—or just for the family.

Robert and I occasionally danced with the kids, but mostly we loved to watch them. Their delight was our joy. We could watch our kids' creativity, spontaneity, and joy for hours—and did.

Because we loved watching the kids perform, they often put together plays and choreographed movements to songs. Bridgette, especially, lived to perform. She sang into a hairbrush or anything that resembled a microphone until we bought her a fake mic. After that, she danced and sang as often as she could.

When the Rock kids came around, the six kids found ways to entertain us as well. We never tired of seeing our kids be creative—unless it was at bedtime!

We also hosted many parties at our house. If we could figure out an event to celebrate, we did! We invited gobs of kids over and put out snacks and soda, and cranked up the jukebox. Halloween parties, birthdays, graduations, or whatever. The moment the kids had a party idea, I said, "Great! Let's do it!" And boy, did we ever do it up.

Surprisingly, even the Los Angeles suburbs can be like small towns. Gossip runs high. People live in the same homes forever. Kids go together to the same schools from elementary through high school graduation. I'd run into friends at the supermarket, Kmart, wherever. And over the years since we'd lived in the apartment in Canoga Park, Fran and I would run into each other and talk, occasionally getting together for cards or dinner. One day, I invited her over for lunch to catch up on life.

By now, Fran's son, Adam Rich, was the darling of the hit television series, *Eight is Enough*, playing the precocious Nicholas Bradford. She never really bragged about Adam, but she, like any proud mother, spoke of how fun it was, and what a good experience it was for him. I enjoyed hearing about him. It all seemed so exciting.

After I cleaned up the lunch dishes, I shared our little news with her. The kids had recently been in my sister Carol's wedding. Kirk, at nine, was her ring bearer. He looked the miniature man in a white tux with a bow tie. My three girls carried flower baskets, all with their happy little faces, rosy cheeks, and wearing white, ruffled floor-length dresses. I had pulled Melissa's hair back in a bun. All three had flower and ribbon barrettes in their hair.

I showed off the pictures to Fran. Her hand went to her throat. "Barb, they're so darling," she gushed. "Would you mind if I showed these pictures to my agent?"

Here it was again. Fran just trying to be nice. I shrugged. "Sure, I guess." I honestly didn't think anything would come of it. Fran had offered so many times to introduce me to the agent, but now *she* removed the first, scary step from my hands. I could let her do that. And maybe once her agent, Iris Burton, declined to see my kids, we could let go of that topic for good.

I guess there was a tiny place inside that thought it might be fun. But my timidity about trying new things alone hadn't changed since high school. I still needed someone to take me by the hand when encountering some huge, new venture. And when Fran offered her hand, I let her take mine and lead me.

Later that night, bowls of ice cream in our hands, the TV on and the kids in bed, I thought about telling Robert. I watched him as he kept his eyes trained on the TV. When a commercial interrupted his show, out came the remote and the images on the screen passed by faster than I could comprehend them.

I thought about my kids being on one of those commercials. Would Robert still flip channel to channel if his kids were on there? I was sure I'd never find out. The photos would return by mail from Fran, a one-word note in her sharp scribble, "SORRY!"

I decided it best not to say anything. I didn't know how he'd react. It seemed silly to say something about an event that was never going to happen.

chapter 6

Iris

Why had I said yes?

The thought ate at me ever since Fran had left with those pictures. Nothing would ever come of it, so why was I stressing? After all, Fran told me, Iris Burton was the biggest name in children's agents. She had about 75 clients, and she thought of them as though they were her own kids. She may have been brusque and abrasive in speech and behavior, but she had a heart of gold. She protected her kids with a fierce mother-bear quality. She knew her stuff and didn't take nothin' from nobody.

Iris had been quoted as saying, "By the time a kid walks through the door, I know if he or she's a winner or a loser. If they jump in or slouch in, if they're biting their nails or rocking back and forth, I don't want 'em. If I don't see the hidden strength, feel the energy, then the magic isn't there. I can smell it like a rat.

"I hate to say it, but kids are pieces of meat. I've never had anything but filet mignon. I've never had hamburger—my kids are the choice meat."

I tried not to think about it. And usually, I was very successful. A busy mom of four kids doesn't have time to think much about the "what ifs" in a future that probably wouldn't even happen. If I thought about it at all, it was more along the lines of, "Why would anyone want my kids?" But it wasn't long until Fran gave me a call. "She wants to see them," Fran said, without even saying hello. "Barb, this is so exciting!"

I smiled at her pleasure. But I still knew it was nothing. I'd take the steps, it would be fun, but most likely wouldn't amount to anything.

That night over a spaghetti dinner, I said to the kids, "Would you like to be on television? Would you like to be on commercials?"

"Okay!" they chorused. "Yeah!"

Bridgette, my little performer, brightened up the most. "Like Adam?"

"Adam's on a series," I said. "So it wouldn't be like that. But remember when he was on commercials?"

I had little sets of blue eyes and brown eyes glued to me. All the little heads nodded.

"It would be like that. We're going to be talking to someone who might help you get on commercials—if you'd like that."

They all said they would, but not with the over-the-top enthusiasm that you might expect from kids. Perhaps they were mirroring my own calmness. At that point, I still did not expect anything to come of this, and even if it did, it would just be something fun, certainly not life-changing.

The next morning, I got the kids off to school. Candace sat at the kitchen table with a coloring book in front of her, laying the colors out in a row. I dug out the piece of paper with IRIS and her phone number printed on it from beneath the pile of papers that had accumulated overnight. I'd been up for hours, but I looked at the clock to be sure it was a reasonable time to call. At just a few minutes after eight, I decided that since most offices open at eight, it might be a good time to catch her.

Instead of the crisp, professional voice I expected, an angry man growled into the phone. "Who is this?"

My heart pounded in my chest. "May I please speak with Iris?"

"What do you want?"

"I'm supposed to call her ... Fran Rich, Adam Rich's mother ..."

A raspy voice burst in the background. "Who is that?" And then, the sound of the phone shifting hands. "Who are you?" the raspy voice shouted.

"I'm Barbara Cameron. Fran Rich told me you wanted me to call ..."

"Honey, what are you doin'?" she interrupted, taking the New York abrasive tone a notch stronger. "What're you calling me at eight o'clock for? Don't you understand? I don't go to bed until two o'clock in the morning. I'm workin' hard. I'm on the phone. I'm doin' this, doin' that. I don't get to sleep until two or three o'clock in the morning. Don't *ever* call me at eight o'clock in the morning. Call me at 11:00. Bye."

Click.

I stared at the receiver, stunned. Slowly, I hung up the phone. I felt like someone had just shot a hundred cups of coffee into me. I trembled a little, and tried to get my mind to accept what I'd just heard. And what should I do with it? That woman scared me to death. Call her at 11:00? Was she serious?

"I'm not calling that woman back," I said to myself, beginning quite a conversation. Leaning on the kitchen counter, I tried to catch my breath. To analyze what happened, and what I should do with it.

"Oh, Barbara, she's a busy woman."

"Yeah. So I heard."

"She was *sleeping*. You're not such a delightful person when you've been wakened from a dead sleep."

"I'm not *that* bad."

"She's a busy woman. Call her."

I grabbed a dust rag and started dusting everything in sight. I transferred one load of laundry from the washer to the dryer and started another load in the washer. I picked up around the house.

"Call her."

I helped Candace find the doll she wanted to play with.

Sighing, I put my hands on my hips. "Okay. So I'll call her. But when? Did she want this to be an appointment? Or did she just mean to call her *around* 11?"

"Who are you talking to, Mommy?" Candace asked.

"Myself."

"Okay," she said happily and skipped away, swinging her doll by its soft arms.

I knew the exact minute the clock said 11. I knew, because I had been checking it every two minutes or so.

I stared at the clock, wondering what to do. I certainly didn't want to get yelled at again! "Should I call her at 11:15? Or maybe wait until 11:30?"

My churning stomach and uptight nerves spurred me to call sooner. "Hello?" I said cautiously, closing my eyes to brace for the assault I was sure was coming. "This is Barbara Cameron."

"Oh, hi, honey. How are you?" Iris said, sweet as could be.

"Great! How are you?" I wondered if she remembered our previous conversation. I decided she'd figure it out sooner or later. With my heart pounding in my throat, I ventured, "I'm really sorry for calling you so early this morning."

"Yeah, honey, well, just don't call me that early in the morning anymore. Why don't you bring the kids in Thursday. Four-thirty."

"Okay," I said, waiting for more information.

Click.

I again stared at the receiver. Took a deep breath. Tried to smile. This was going to be fun, right? I sighed again.

What have I gotten myself into?

Thursday I dressed the kids in their Kmart-special clothes. Kirk wore jeans and a striped shirt, his bowl-cut hair brushed and shiny. The girls wore simple dresses. I curled Candace's and Melissa's hair, and styled Bridgette's short, superfine cottony hair with a little flip at the ends. When Robert got home from work, we all climbed into our VW bus.

I didn't feel comfortable driving the Los Angeles freeways. I hadn't been "over the hill" to Hollywood much in my life. Robert, always the man of the house, took over the driving. I was glad to have him with us. He could be the man in front while I, hopefully, could hide behind him. He was my strength, my voice.

Robert stopped the car about an hour later in front of a large, two-story home in the Hollywood Hills. Bridgette chattered most of the way, excited about the opportunity to become a real actress. Kirk stared out the window, trying to do the impossible—separate himself from the girls. Melissa and Candace listened to Bridgette, looked out the window, and didn't say much.

"Be on your best behavior," I said to them before they opened the car doors.

"You know how to behave," Robert said sternly. "And," he added with a wink, "if you're good, I'll stop at McDonald's for ice cream later."

The kids had long ago learned that Daddy meant what he said. He could be fierce or funny, and no matter what it was he said, he stood by it.

Together we walked up the pathway through a perfectly manicured landscape. Normally talkative, witty Robert had nothing to say, so I knew this large house indicating money, as well as the situation, intimidated him as much as it did me.

We knocked on a pair of French doors. "Come in!" Iris called. My heart melted at the sound of her voice. I tried not to look as nervous as I felt. Robert opened the door. I stepped through first, then the children following in order of their age, Robert trailing behind, closing the door gently.

Iris sat behind a large mahogany desk talking on the phone. A cigarette dangled out of one side of her mouth, bouncing as she spoke. She motioned for us to sit on the sofa across from her desk. The children sat and kept very still. Photos of Iris's very famous clients adorned all the walls of her office. Bridgette saw Adam's picture and elbowed Kirk and pointed. The kids seemed absorbed in looking at the photos. I noticed the unattended assistant's desk off to one side, then looked back at Iris. She appeared to be in her late 40s, and dressed very casually in gray cashmere sweats. Her dark, shoulder-length hair was nicely combed. She was wearing just a touch of makeup. She didn't look near as harsh as she'd sounded on the phone with me. And the person she spoke with on the phone now had the all-business Iris. I wondered if there was any other way for her.

She hung up and took us all in. She looked at Kirk. She pointed at him. "Okay, honey, come over here. I want you to stand in front of me."

Kirk obediently got up from the sofa and walked to her desk. He put his hands in his pockets, his shoulders hunched just enough for a mother—or an agent—to notice. He didn't take his eyes off her. I hoped he wouldn't turn to his father and make a comment about her smoking.

Iris looked him over. "I want you to say this line: 'Hey, Mom, let's go to McDonald's.'" She said it without any inflection whatsoever.

Kirk said obediently, "Hey, Mom, let's go to McDonald's."

"Okay, honey. Now say it with more energy."

I leaned forward on the sofa, urging him on silently. I knew he could do it. I knew if he just felt comfortable, he would come out of his shell. I hoped that by having Mom and Dad behind him, he would feel safe and open up.

"Hey, Mom, let's go to McDonald's."

Iris and Kirk continued to stay in eye contact. "Now say, 'Wow, look at those Hot Wheels go.'"

The stiffness eased. "Wow, look at those Hot Wheels go."

"Okay. Sit down. You. Come on up here."

Bridgette popped off the sofa. She bounced over to the desk, every part of her wiggling. Her easy smile took over her face. I knew, without looking, that her eyes lit up. It was her chance to shine, and she knew it. And shine she did. "Hey, Mom, let's go to McDonald's."

Delivered like a pro.

Iris said, "Now say, 'Isn't Barbie pretty?'"

Without hesitation, and with equal gusto, Bridgette said, "Isn't Barbie pretty?" She had such a great personality, and every bit of it came shining through.

Great job! I wanted to tell her. I applauded inside, wishing I could do so outside.

"You," Iris pointed to Melissa.

Melissa walked to the desk and stood with her hands clasped in front of her. She looked darling with her curled hair and pink dress. Iris had her go through the same routine as Bridgette, delivering her lines as asked. Melissa lacked Bridgette's charisma, but gave a decent delivery of the lines. Not spectacular. Nothing exciting.

Iris called Candace up. She swiveled from side to side, looking up at Iris with her large, blue eyes.

When Candace sat down, without any preface, Iris pointed to the kids one by one, skipping Bridgette. "I'll take him and give him a try for a year. I'll take her. Bring the little one back in a year; she's too young."

I wasn't sure I heard right. "What about Bridgette?"

"Nope." Sharp. Blunt.

"Why?"

"Nope."

We just stood there, wondering. What are we supposed to do now?

Thoughts raced through my head. "Do you want me to get pictures?" I blurted.

"I don't need pictures. But if you want pictures, go ahead."

I knew very little about this business, but one thing I did know was that everybody has pictures—headshots—for the casting directors to look at.

"Could I take my own pictures?"

"Yeah, sure, I don't care. Just send some to me."

A woman knocked on the office door and came in with her two daughters.

"Okay, thank you very much," Robert and I said, a little stunned.

"See you, honey. I'll call you."

And that was that.

As we walked to the car, I felt a mother's joy and sadness all at once. I was glad for Melissa and Kirk. But what about Bridgette? She was the one I'd finally done this for. She was the one who had her heart set on being on television. And to have no answer from Iris as to *why*. She'd been to the point and wasted no words.

I supposed that whatever Kirk had done in front of her caused her to take notice. She liked his look. He may not have said the lines well, but there was something in him. He had listened well, and he followed directions. Did what she asked him to do. Looked her in the eye with that coy look that didn't hide his clever spirit. I was certain she could tell he was bright. And I realized that at the moment she dismissed him, I knew she was going to take him. And that she'd dealt with Bridgette differently. I had hoped I was wrong, but I knew whatever delightful personality Bridgette had, she lacked the look Hollywood wanted.

Once we got into the VW bus, Bridgette spoke up. "Why not me, Mommy? Why didn't she pick me?"

My heart broke for her right there. I tried to look at her as an outsider might. Bridgette was cute, but didn't seem to have whatever Iris was looking for. A character actor, perhaps. The rejection grieved me. My precious little girl. And I had to give her an answer without crushing her. "Sweetie, think about the commercials we see. All the little girls have blue eyes and long, blond hair. Yours is very short. We will wait until it grows longer. We will have to wait until your braces come off and then we'll come back and audition again for Iris, okay? You did a *great* job. I'm so proud of you."

"I'm SO PROUD of you!" Robert nearly sang in one of his funny voices. "What did that lady have all of you say back there?"

"Hey, Mom! Let's go to McDonald's!" all the kids said in unison.

"Well, ohhh-kay then!" Robert said, and we all went to McDonald's for the promised ice cream.

chapter 7

A Room Full of Clones

I didn't expect to hear from Iris for a long time. I knew from Fran how this business worked. We had verbally agreed to a one-year commitment with Iris. This meant that we *must* go on *every* audition she sent us to. We couldn't decide which ones we'd like to do, and couldn't say no if we were just having an off day. Soon I would receive contracts stating this, among other things, as well as a percentage Iris would earn off every booking. I also knew that auditions could come either fast and furious, or, more likely, slow and well-spaced.

"This is going to be fun!" I told the two who would be auditioning. If it ever gets to be something you don't want to do, you can stop. BUT! We are telling Iris that we'll try it for a year. That means that no matter what, we're agreeing to a year. Is that understood?"

They understood commitments, having been involved in t-ball, soccer, and dance in the past.

Bridgette seemed to accept the explanation I had given her about why Iris probably hadn't chosen her. Her always upbeat outlook served her well, and she was excited for her siblings.

Within a week we had our first call—for Kirk. "Friday at 3:55. Baker Nesbit," Iris rasped. And then she gave me the address.

"Okay," I said. "Hold on a sec. I need to get something to write on."

"What? Why don't you have a pencil and paper by your phone? What do you think I am, anyway? You think I got all the time in the world?"

I grabbed an envelope, flipped it over and wrote with a pencil that needed sharpening. "How do I get there?"

"What do you think? I'm a travel agent, too? I'm not a travel agent," Iris yelled, my stomach tying a few more knots. "You got a *Thomas Guide*? Get a *Thomas Guide* and get yourself there. If I had to tell everybody where they had to go, and every corner where they needed to turn, I wouldn't get my work done."

Click.

Feeling properly chastised, and totally embarrassed, I went to the car and got out my ratty *Thomas Guide* that had been stuffed under the back seat. I looked up the address in the index, found the place, and mapped out my directions, still feeling a little shaky from being humiliated by Iris. I vowed to never be without pencil and paper by the phone ever again. To never ask another unnecessary question. I would be the best mother Iris dealt with. Fran had told me about some of the strange things mothers did, and had heard Iris complain about them. I didn't want to be the stage mother, the mother who caused problems. I wanted to be the responsible parent. I wanted her to be proud of me, to like me because I didn't ask her a bunch of questions. I decided that I would always get my kids to their auditions on time. I would learn how my kids and I needed to act to be professional, and we would do that.

By dinner time, I had gotten rid of those awful feelings about being a bad person and a bad mother, and spilled over with excitement.

"Guess what?" I said, sitting down to a simple dinner of turkey tacos. "Kirk's going on an audition!"

The news created a rousing cheer in our family circle.

"Don't you think it's exciting?"

"I think it's very cool," Robert said, reaching over to give Kirk a good guy-to-guy gentle slug on the arm. "Way to go."

Kirk leaned over his plate, tucking a folded taco in his mouth. He looked up, chewing, considering. "What am I supposed to do?" he asked.

"Don't talk with your mouth full," Robert ordered. "Have good manners. That's what you do."

"Fran said that you'll stand in front of a camera, say your name, how old you are, and who your agent is. Then you'll say your lines."

"What lines?"

"We pick them up at the audition."

While Robert did the dishes, I called Fran a second time, just to have someone be excited with me. I called Patty Rock and told her, too. Every part of me wanted to jump up and down and shout. But really, this was just an audition. I'd heard of kids going on fifty auditions before they got a booking. And some never did. The thought sobered me that we could be at this for a year and never have a booking.

Friday I waited outside of Kirk's elementary school in the VW bus. I had the directions scribbled out in a notebook, a fresh shirt for Kirk, and butterflies spinning in my stomach. I had a cassette of oldies in the tape deck, hoping their bouncy rhythms would keep up with my nerves, giving me something to do while I waited.

Kirk saw me, waved, and trotted out to the car. "Hey, Mom."

"Hey. How was school today?"

"Fine."

I rarely got more feedback than that, so I was used to it. We drove with '50s music as our background. "Are you nervous?"

Kirk shrugged, not looking at me.

"Do you think it will be fun?"

He shrugged again.

Nine-year-old boys, I thought, and turned up the music and sang along.

The drive took longer than I thought, but I'd allowed plenty of time. We were at least an hour early, and for that I was glad.

I drove by the building twice making sure it was the correct one. I noted the car wash next door as a landmark for future auditions, and looked for a place to park. There weren't any spots along the curb available, so around the block we went again. Driving through the residential area, I still couldn't find any parking.

My stomach stormed with nerves. My lack of parallel parking ability, combined with the busy street, made such a maneuver too terrifying for me to try. After driving by the building a third time, I gave up and parked in the Norm's Restaurant parking lot across the street. I threw the car into park and took a deep breath. "Okay, kiddo. Let's go."

Inside the building, a security guard directed us down a plain hallway to a door marked "Casting Director." We opened the door,

Kirk's school picture at Nevada Elementary School.

and the sight so startled me, stealing the excitement and happy nervousness away. There, in a large room, sat at least twenty nine-year-old boys, blond hair, bowl cut. I felt like I'd stepped into a room with Kirk clones. Mothers of all shapes and sizes sat with their boys. Some spoke with one another, some only spoke to their boys in soft voices, others spoke so loudly that it seemed as though they *wanted* to be heard by the others.

A clipboard sat on top of a counter, and I signed us in. A stack of papers sat next to it with the lines Kirk was supposed to memorize and say in front of the camera. *Sides*, Fran had called them. "You'll find the sides near the sign-in sheet. Take one, and practice with Kirk."

Kirk and I took the last available seats and began to practice his lines. "Well, Timmy," I chirped with great intonation, inflection, and exaggeration, "what is *that* you're eating?"

Kirk looked at me and said flatly, "Life cereal. I love it."

"Say it with more excitement," I urged. "More energy."

"Life cereal. I love it." He sounded like a sick female.

Yeah, my kid was an actor all right.

It seemed forever before he was called into the casting office. I waited impatiently, not knowing where to look or what to say — or not.

"My Joey is going to Kellogg's this afternoon," a woman sang out to another across the room. "Did you get a call for that audition, too?"

The other woman's face fell. I could see Joey's mother's face perked up a little.

"No, we didn't get that call."

"Too bad," the first woman said, not sounding as though she thought it was too bad at all.

The door opened, and a boy who looked vaguely familiar entered with his mother. The collective air in the room seemed to depress quite a bit. The woman next to me breathed, "Great. Ryan's here. We might as well all go home."

"Ryan?" I asked her.

"He gets all the parts. If he's here, he'll probably land the part." She pushed her fingers through her short, dark hair, her lips almost in a pout. "I don't know why I come to these things. It's pointless."

A tall, willowy blonde, dressed in a figure-hugging cotton dress made a big show of sighing, looking at her watch, then moving toward the phone on a desk. She dialed a number, considered her fingernails while she waited. "Oh, hi. Brian? This is Simone. Yes, I wondered if you have anything else for Scott this afternoon."

Pause. All adult eyes in the room were trained on her.

"Yes. I'm here at Baker Nesbit." She took the pencil from the sign-in sheet, grabbed one of the sides and flipped it over. "Sure, we can make it. Where? ABC? For a possible TV movie? Why, sure!"

She waved her hand in the air, as if trying to attract any attention she didn't already have. "Having the sides ahead of time doesn't matter. Scott can memorize *so* quickly. He'll come through for you. Thank you! Buh-bye!" She hung up the phone and swung back to her seat. "Why, Scott, honey, you have another audition this afternoon. For a *movie*! Isn't that exciting? They asked specifically for *you*."

Some of the other kids had gathered around Ryan. He held himself in such a way that it seemed he thought of himself as rather special—like he was holding court for his subjects. He talked to some of the kids as though he knew them and were friends. Other boys tried to get his attention and were ignored.

I wanted to gag.

Kirk came out of the room, and the next boy was called.

The moment we left the building, I started pelting him with questions. "What was it like? How did you do? What do you think?"

"I did okay, I guess."

"Do you think you'll get a callback?"

He looked at me in the way only preadolescent boys can do. A look that says you are about as smart as a lizard. "I don't know."

He didn't get a callback.

The next five auditions went about the same. It was like a replay of the first, only with a different cast of characters. A room filled with Kirk-clones, pompous mothers, hopeful mothers, arrogant and braggart mothers. Only now I noticed that every time a kid walked through that door to the inner sanctum—a place where no parent was ever allowed—that all ears trained toward the door, straining to hear what went on behind it. If the kid was new, no one really paid attention—except that kid's mother. She tried to listen through the door, hoping to catch a few words her child was saying. If the child was known to snag a lot of parts, everyone tried to listen. All the bodies leaned toward the door as if a stiff wind had come up, blowing everyone that direction. And as the kids walked out the door, everyone glanced over to observe his face. The degree of glow, or lack of it, gave the remaining parents some thought as to where their own son might stand in the ratings.

Sometimes, a boy would come out, quite excited and saying, "They're going to call me back, Mom!" His mother would do any form of congratulating that made certain everyone in the room knew *her* son was getting a callback. The worst was when the boy would burst through the door shouting, "I got it! I got it!" The rest of us wondered why they didn't just dismiss us at that moment. Sometimes they did, sometimes they didn't.

After a handful of these auditions, I'd had it with the atmosphere that oozed a sense that a kid's personal value was based on whether or not they had auditions. Or whether or not he got a part, or many parts. I hated hearing moms brag as though that made them better than the rest of us. From that point on, I signed in, took the sides, and removed my child from the room. We practiced the sides in the hallway, an empty room, anywhere but in that snake's nest. My children didn't need to see that or be a part of it. Besides, I thought that letting them audition in their own voices, rather than adapting the voice of someone they heard around them, would be best for them. Then they would book or not book on their own merit.

Melissa began being called out on auditions, as well. When I was by myself, I'd talk to God in a casual, anticipatory sort of way. "God, it would be *so cool* if they would book just one commercial. Just one! Please, Lord? If I could just see their little faces on TV. Please." I

Robert and Barbara in 1979—the year Kirk began to act in commercials.

hoped with all my heart that God would hear and answer me. But I really didn't think anything would happen. It was a fun dream, something exciting to think about—but one I knew had little chance of coming true. And that was okay for me. It really was. This was a fun diversion for the kids and me—something we could do together. We couldn't afford much on Robert's small teacher's salary, but gas money and time I had.

On the sixth audition, held in a park, Kirk had a meltdown. Tired, hungry, worn out from not really knowing what he was supposed to do, he started to cry when he was supposed to deliver his lines.

The casting director came to see me. "He'll be okay," I encouraged. "He gets shy and overwhelmed when he doesn't know what he's supposed to do. If you just give him clear directions, he'll do it."

The director of the commercial took Kirk aside and threw a baseball with him for a couple minutes, getting him loosened up and his mind off the pressure. I have no idea why he would be so kind, when so many other kids didn't cry. But that was all Kirk needed. The next time they sat him down with a bowl of cereal, trained the camera on him, and asked him to say his lines, he did it perfectly—and landed the job!

The news of the booking came through Iris. "Congratulations. Kirk got the Cocoa Puffs commercial. He needs to show up for work on Wednesday, 8:00, Griffith Park at the Pecan Grove picnic area. You'll have a wardrobe call tomorrow."

I wrote it down, kept my voice in check. "Thank you, Iris. He'll be there." I hung up the phone and screamed, "Whoo-hoo!!!"

Robert didn't think much of it. "That's cool. But Barb, it's just one job."

"Robert," I pleaded for him to get excited with me, "he's going to be on a *commercial*."

"When he makes $10,000, then I'll think it's something real and worthwhile."

His down-to-earth attitude didn't stop me from soaring this time. I was so excited. "Thank you, Lord!" I said, praying as I puttered around the house.

Kirk did great. The producer loved him. I was so excited, I made a batch of my secret-recipe chocolate chip cookies and brought a basket of them to the set as a thank-you to all the cast and crew for letting my boy be a part of this amazing event. I had no idea they would be so excited that an actor's mom would take the time to bake cookies for them. It was one of the many lessons I would learn about kindness along the way. Their obvious gratitude for what they saw as my thoughtfulness spawned in me a plan: no matter how many

Kirk filming a commercial with James Garner.

bookings my children may receive, I would always bring a batch of my cookies as a thank-you for the cast and crew's hard work.

Sometimes commercials get cancelled for one reason or another, and that's what happened to Kirk's first one. I was disappointed. He'd made it this far. I couldn't stand it! So close, but still not close enough. I didn't hesitate to ask God for yet another favor. "God, it was so cool that Kirk got a booking … but it never aired. Can you get him just one more commercial? It was so fun. And I'd love to see him on TV." I could hear the tiny whine in my voice, but it was really more like a little girl, pleading for something she really, really wanted.

I got to be a pro at this audition thing. I had a notebook where I kept track of *everything*: how to get to the studios, what each one was like, what they wanted. I wrote down what the kids wore to auditions so if they got a callback, they could wear the exact same thing, their hair styled the exact same way. Fran had warned me how critical it was to make sure that my children looked identical as the first time they were seen. "This way, they remember your child better. They can see up to 300 kids for one commercial. If you dress them exactly the same, they might remember why they liked them. And it might be that they liked the look they had in those clothes and in that hairstyle."

So, if Kirk wore a belt and had on tennis shoes and white socks, I wrote that down. If Melissa had braids and pink ribbons in her hair, I put pink ribbons in her braided hair. Everything got written down and kept track of.

I learned what I needed to do, and learned fast. I eavesdropped on the other mothers whenever I could, soaking up information like a sponge. As a result, we learned what was critical and put those things into practice: my kids were on time, they were professional, they did what they needed to do, which, in turn, made Iris look good. I loved it when I heard Iris had gotten feedback from the casting director, "Oh, yeah, the Cameron kids are great. The mother's great."

Shortly after our cancelled commercial disappointment, Kirk booked He-man and 409 commercials. The 409 stayed on the television for quite some time, earning him some recognition.

People started to call our house. "Was that Kirk I saw on TV?"

"Yes," I said, trying to sound as though it was no big deal.

"I saw Kirk!" another would proclaim.

"Isn't it exciting?"

I could barely believe it myself. This was *real*. There my little boy was—*on TV!*

The advertising company told me on the day of filming that they would provide me with a list of when the commercial would air. I'd sit with a blank tape in the VCR, remote in hand, ready to press "record" the moment the commercial began. I'd tape it over and over, even though I already had plenty of copies of it. Eventually, I would just watch. Often they played during soap operas, talk shows, and game shows. I saw more TV during that period of our lives!

Every time I saw him, my heart nearly exploded with joy, excitement, and pride. My shy little boy opened up and became someone else in the commercial. And he had such fun working on them.

In the evenings, when the kids and Robert were home, if one came on, the shout would go out, "Kirk's on!" and the whole gang came running. We'd shout and scream and be delighted every time. The girls loved to see their big brother on TV and never once seemed to be jealous.

Melissa also booked a commercial for Valley National Bank in Arizona, but it wasn't aired locally. I was sad I wouldn't have the chance to see hers air. Twice she got close to booking a series, but didn't pass the final callback. She even had the unique job of being a body model for clothes made for seven-year-olds. They would fit the clothing to her body in the design stage.

Over time, she realized she didn't like being in front of a camera or the harsh criticism of the casting directors. She loved being on the set, but felt awkward, shy, and uncomfortable in front of the camera. So after a few years of giving it a valiant effort, she came to me. "Mom, I don't want to do this anymore."

"It's okay for you to stop, but are you sure?"

"I'm sure," she said.

"You'll have to tell Iris."

Melissa's eyes grew wide. "She scares me."

"I know, she scares me, too, honey," I said, trying to assure her that I felt the same way. I knew that Iris would be wonderful to Melissa and respect her decision, and also knew this tough call would be a good character-building experience. "Telling her yourself is the right thing to do."

And so she did.

After Melissa and Kirk put in a year, Candace stood in front of Iris as a five-year-old, and Iris took her this time. Kirk was working plenty of commercials, and was now the kid the roomful of boys and mothers hated to see arrive. But I still refused to become involved in the audition-room politics and one-upmanship games. "You are no better than anyone else," I told my kids often. "You treat everyone the same. No one is better than anyone else."

Because Kirk was working in commercials rather steadily by now, Iris wanted to move him into more theatrical roles, including television series, television movies of the week, and feature films. She suggested taking him to acting classes to help him make this transition from commercials. I enrolled him in a group called Young Actors' Space. After Kirk had attended about six classes, Diane Harden, the owner and coach, pulled me aside and told me she didn't feel Kirk needed the instruction. "He's a natural!" she said. And that was the last acting class he ever took.

Kirk had far surpassed the $10,000 mark his father had said would convince him that this was a worthwhile endeavor. But still, Robert pooh-poohed the business. "The kids need to go to college. Sure, this is fun. A nice diversion. An extracurricular activity that also happens to make them money. But, as Iris says, 'Fame is fleeting,' and they'd better have something to fall back on after they're no longer cute little kids on commercials."

I knew Robert was right. But did a kid need to go to college to be happy? "What if the girls just want to get married and have families? They don't need college for that."

"Everyone needs to go to college," Robert countered. "Without college, you can't get anywhere in life. You can't depend on our daughters marrying someone and being supported their whole lives. What if they don't get married? They need to find something to support themselves, and college is the only way that they will be respected and able to get good jobs."

I clammed up, not wanting to argue with Robert. What did I know about going to college? Maybe he knew something I didn't. I thought about the "what ifs" like he wanted me to, but knew that the girls would find something that interested them whether it was through going to college or not. College wasn't for everyone.

Honestly, I put a lot of guilt on myself for not going to college. I felt stupid that I didn't have a lot of knowledge about worldly things. I mean, I had only graduated from high school while Robert was a graduate of the University of Southern California with a master's degree. So I looked to Robert because I felt I was stupid, and needed him to be smart for me.

But that didn't stop me from continuing to shuttle the kids to auditions. Nor did it stop me from praying, "Lord, the commercials are great, but can we have a bit part on a TV show? Or in a movie? That would be so cool."

chapter 8

Opening Doors

Life took on a stuttering familiarity. Some days we'd have auditions, and I would wait outside school. The kids knew if my car was there, they had auditions. And auditions became so routine, boring, and tiring, that they often didn't want to go. We'd made our commitment to Iris, and so we had to honor that commitment to go on every audition we were sent to. I tried to instill excitement into them. "How was your day at school? Are you hungry? We can stop at McDonald's for a snack."

Auditions may have been painful, and the kids may have hated them (who wouldn't hate feeling like one of the cattle in the herd — they dub it a "cattle call" for a reason), but they *loved* acting and interacting with the people they met on the sets. They were a blast.

Whenever I could, I'd take all the kids with me on the set. And everyone was so nice to all my kids, not just the one who had the job. I taught them to look at adults, to speak clearly, and to treat everyone the same. Stars and cameramen. Producers and grips. All are equal.

When I wasn't visiting with those around me, I sat on a chair and knitted or worked on my needlework. It was a great way to pass the time, and easy to stop what I was doing to watch the takes. I felt so proud, watching my children take direction well. Much of the work of acting is taking good direction. If you can do what you're asked to do, you are a treasure for the director, word gets around, and soon you're invited to more auditions. More auditions allow the chance for more work. And so, my kids had many auditions, sometimes as many as three times a week. Then, if they booked, there was the time spent on the set—one to three days for each commercial.

Robert and I had many conversations about this. To Robert, it remained a fantasy, not something real and valuable. I saw it as a different kind of education for the kids. Kirk and Candace had been identified by the school system as "gifted." And, as gifted kids, they needed more mental challenge and stimulation. Acting gave this to them.

"I still want them to go to college," Robert repeated like a skipping record in our jukebox.

"I know. But things are going well, and they keep booking." I leaned forward, hoping he'd really hear me. "I'd like them to take this as far as they can." *And God isn't saying no*, I thought to myself.

Robert shrugged. "I don't want it interfering with the family life."

"Is it now?" I asked, already knowing the answer.

Robert thought a moment. I could see him going over how things had changed in his mind—as well as how they hadn't. "No. But the minute it does, that's it."

"I totally agree. Family is more important than anything."

Robert looked at me as though looking into my heart. "I know it is, darlin'. I just don't want us to lose that. Once these kids have an end to their acting—and it *will* end—I want them to have something to fall back on. College. Family."

"I promise you—and we'll tell the kids—the minute this takes them over, we're done. If it goes to their heads, if they start being snobby ..."

"I do NOT want them ruling the roost the way we've seen other child actors do."

I knew what he meant. It didn't take much to see these little miniature tyrants snapping their fingers and all the adults come running. It was sickening. Even parents and siblings reacted to their selfish demands. "Me either, Robert. You and I may not agree on a lot of things, but we do agree on that."

"I want us to still have dinner together every night. No matter what."

"Will you help?"

Robert considered this as well. "You know I do. And I will."

Robert *did* help. He took half the load. He did laundry, made dinner if we were on a shoot. He did the dishes. He took the kids to school and picked up the ones who weren't working that day. He helped whoever was home with their homework.

It was around that time when we realized that taking Kirk and Candace to auditions and the resulting shoots was becoming a full-time job. And we couldn't afford the extra expenses adding up.

"We have to do something," Robert said one evening after we'd sent the kids to bed with "Happy trails to you!" We had our bowls of ice cream. I sat on the sofa next to him, my feet curled up beneath me.

"I've been thinking," I said, and then scooped a spoonful of Rocky Road into my mouth. I let it melt before continuing. "You've got their earnings in trust …"

Robert nodded. After Jackie Coogan, a child star who made hundreds of thousands of dollars, lost all he had because his parents spent it all on goodies for themselves, a law was put in place that a certain percentage of a child's earnings had to go into a trust for him. Robert had voluntarily increased the mandatory percentage, and wisely upped the age at which they would receive the money. Too many child stars went crazy and spent all their money when it landed in their eighteen-year-old hands.

"… but legally, some of their money can be spent on a manager. Children can't get themselves to and from auditions or tapings, and need to have an adult present at all times. So I just thought that maybe I should …" I almost felt bad saying it. But I knew if I didn't do this, I'd have to get a full-time job. We simply could not survive all the added expenses on Robert's meager salary. We didn't spend frivolously, but just the incidentals for the kids being "in the business" was taking its toll. We had to pay union dues, agent fees, taxes, and for photo shoots. We had been keeping all their money in a separate checking account, paying for those items from their earnings. We'd also kept a very close account of every dollar. We found it critical to make sure that we always had the attitude that this was money the kids had earned, not us.

"You want to be their manager," Robert said.

"Yes. If I don't do it, I'll have to get a job, and we'll have to hire someone else to be their manager. What do you think?"

"What does a manager make?"

"A percentage of their income."

"Is it enough?"

"It would be right now." I took another huge mound of ice cream and let it cool me off from the hot San Fernando Valley summer.

"Whatever we need to do to make it official, let's do it."

From then on, it got easier. I took this on as any job—with full gusto and determination. I found, however, that it was difficult for Kirk to see me as "Mom" when we were at home, and "Manager" when we were working. The difference in how I acted in the home and on the set was unnerving and difficult for him. So, I decided that I would put on different "hats" to make it clear which person he was dealing with at any given time. At home, I wore jeans, sweats, and "Mom" clothes. At work, I put on clothing more suited to a casual manager: soft skirts, slacks, blouses, and so on. Nothing fancy, but just a step up from the home gear.

At home, there were days when I saw a glimmer of what our marriage might be like. Laughter, fun, closeness. And then, some event would jar my reality.

Rusty invited Robert to come to his twenty-year high school reunion. They had graduated one year apart, so it could be a really fun party with lots of people Robert and Rusty knew. I spent a lot of time thinking about what dress to wear, and finally found something that made me feel nice. Nothing too revealing, just a flattering dress.

We sat at a table with two other couples. The guys were all former high school friends. I sat between Robert and Rusty. On the other side of Robert sat a blonde bombshell. This gorgeous woman wore a slinky dress cut into a slicing V that showed more than I cared to see. She immediately took to Robert, cooing, batting her eyelashes, her face bright and responsive to everything Robert said. The two laughed and talked, sometimes almost as if they were telling secrets.

I, on the other hand, had the great view of Robert's back. As the evening wore on, I was beside myself. I smiled to everyone else, pretending that everything was fine, and being the good wife who isn't jealous and doesn't take things wrong. Inside there was screaming in my head. *Am I crazy? Am I really seeing this? Could my husband*

really be this insensitive? Am I that boring that he can't talk to me at all? What's going on?

I tried to remind myself that he needed validation and attention as we all do.

The battle raged inside, while the outside of Barbara looked fine and content.

The crowd called for Robert and Rusty to get on stage and put on a hand-to-hand balancing show. It didn't take any coercion to get these two showoffs up there. During their impromptu performance,

Ms. Bombshell jumped from her chair, cheering, applauding, and shouting at how fabulous they were.

I stared, stunned.

When Robert returned to the table, soaking up Ms. Bombshell's gushing remarks, I stood and walked quietly to the bathroom to have a good cry. The other woman at the table, Ms. Bombshell's sister-in-law, entered a moment after my tears started.

"Am I crazy?" I asked her. "Am I seeing things right? Is my husband really so engrossed in another woman?"

"You're not crazy," the woman told me, fishing in her purse, then handing me a fresh tissue. "She does this to all the men. I apologize for her. It's not right."

The event ended, and Robert asked, "Honey, what's wrong?"

My mouth gaped. "You don't know?"

"What? Her? Oh, come on, Barb. She doesn't mean anything. It's nothing."

I gave him a look.

"Don't let it bug you. You're being ridiculous here, Barb."

Maybe I would have thought I was ridiculous had it not been for the sister-in-law's confirmation.

At the hotel elevators, we ran into the rest of the group again. Ms. Bombshell proceeded to give hugs all around. Then, when she got to Robert, she planted a passionate kiss on his lips.

The elevator doors opened and Robert and I stepped inside, alone. I communicated in the only way I knew how—I clammed up. I shut down so well that I blocked out everything else good that could have happened that night.

I continued praying softly, almost talking to myself when I was alone. I admit, they were selfish prayers. "Lord, help my kids to be happy. Help me to be a good mom. And God, if one of my kids could just be in a movie, that would be so *cool*. I mean, I'm grateful for the commercials, but a *movie* ... now that would be special." I prayed for my quietly deteriorating relationship with Robert.

Life changed, and yet it didn't.

We still had Sundays with the Rocks and other friends and family members at Santa Monica beach. We did absolutely everything we could with the family. We had dinner together every night. We had the Rocks over and we talked while the kids hung out in the backyard and played together. Our extended family—the grandparents, aunts, uncles, and cousins—also came over as they had before. Robert drove the kids crazy by singing the entire "Happy trails to you!" song or "The Party's Over ..." every single night to signal bedtime, and "tooted" reveille each morning to signal wake-up time.

Bridgette : I told my husband that the singing, humming, or whistling of "Happy Trails" is NOT allowed in our house—EVER.

Kirk : They would sing the song, the kids would protest, Dad would threaten to ground or spank us. I'd tiptoe to the door of the hallway and see the truth—that's when all the fun was over for the kids and about to begin for the parents; they broke out ice cream, and started cracking jokes and having a great time—without us.

The chore chart still hung on the wall and all the kids had to do their chores each day, checking them off when they were done.

Melissa : The only thing I hated about my siblings being in the business was that they didn't have to do their chores. If they'd worked all day, then they didn't have to do the chores because they were too tired. They probably were, but I didn't care. I just didn't think it was fair.

The kids could have friends over, but we discouraged them from going elsewhere.

We wanted to know where our kids were at all times and who they were with. So our house was the gathering place. Ours was the party house. Ours was the one kids hung out at on Saturdays.

There were things that did change. Robert had always helped the girls with their math homework, because I didn't feel I could do it. But now, he was the sole parent at home some afternoons, in charge of all homework supervision. He still took them to school and picked them up. But sometimes the burden of making dinner was on them. The good thing was, we all *loved* turkey tacos. No one ever got tired of them. So once Kirk and Candace began to work more regularly, turkey tacos became a staple at our house. We'd have them four or five times a week. No one minded. They were simple, easy to cook, great to eat, and easy to clean up. Any of the kids could make them. And everyone had his or her own special version. Everyone made them different; some open, like a tostada. Robert drenched his in Italian dressing. Some used salsa, some ketchup.

Kirk : Whenever someone would ask, "What are we having for dinner?" we were always hoping the answer was turkey tacos, and disappointed if it wasn't.

Candace : We have them at least twice a week now in our family.

Melissa : So do we! I still love them.

Bridgette : John and I have turkey tacos at least three or four times a week. I'm always saying, "We don't have to have turkey tacos so much." And John says, "They are SO good!" I just laugh. Come on! It's turkey, lettuce, tomatoes, and cheese on a flour tortilla. How can that be so great?

Our family still played games like Battleship, Clue, and Monopoly together.

And Robert still fought with the girls over so many things. He didn't like that they were a little overweight. So he made them do exercises and keep a chart of their weight. If they didn't lose two pounds a week, they were grounded. He wouldn't let them eat ice cream, or any fun food.

And the battles waged over the homework hurt me so. I didn't feel I could challenge him more than I did. Bridgette didn't learn as quickly as the other kids. She struggled so much in school. Her father hated that. He ranted and raved and called her unspeakable names. He got frustrated when she didn't "get" the concepts he was trying to explain. Sometimes he thought she was just being stubborn.

My mother's heart again broke for Bridgie. She had the sweetest, most joyful attitude that I'd known in a child. Even though she felt crushed by her father, she still came out of it sparkling.

Robert was a very good father with solid rules and values. He was just so harsh when those were broken. We had many fights about his harshness. He didn't see how harsh he was being, or how hard of a sledgehammer it was on our girls. The more I heard him say mean things, the further I withdrew from him. Where was the oneness I so desperately wanted? Where was the emotional intimacy? Listening to him be harsh with the girls, and also with me, the seeds were planted: when Candace reached eighteen, I would end the marriage.

We took camping trips in the summer when we could. For a while, we owned an old tent trailer and pulled it behind our Pinto. We took a trip to Truckee to camp, and when I opened the tent, it was *full* of bugs. "ROBERT!" I screamed. "I've had it with this stupid trailer. We are NOT using it EVER again!"

After that, we took our VW bus. We put foam in the back that I covered with material. The kids could lie down back there to nap, play with toys, read, or play cards with each other. We listened to tapes of very old songs, the whole family singing at the tops of our lungs. Or we'd put in stories on tapes and listen to those.

The kids loved their father's sense of humor. He'd say, "Okay everyone. Rest stop ahead!" Everyone got on the alert. Then the moment we were at the sign, he would say, "All right everyone … RRRRRRREST!" And we'd all tilt our heads to one side and close our eyes to "rest."

Occasionally we would stop at a rest stop, and Robert would take his PE teacher's whistle and blow commands. Jumping jacks.

Kirk and James Garner on the set of Bret Maverick.

Kirk was cast as "Boy #1" on the series, Bret Maverick.

Kirk with Cloris Leachman in the TV movie, The Woman Who Willed a Miracle.

Knee bends. Side bends. Running around the buildings. It got the kinks out in an orderly fashion, and was terribly fun for the kids.

Kirk had been doing commercials for about a year when we got the exciting call that he had booked a bit part on the TV show, *Bret Maverick*. The only problem is, we got the call while driving home from a vacation in Chicago. So Kirk and I flew home while Robert and the girls visited Mt.

On the set of Beyond Witch Mountain.

Rushmore and other interesting places we'd hoped to see together along the way.

Bret Maverick was a period television series, set in the Wild West. Kirk was cast as "Boy #1" and had the opportunity to work with James Garner. For his first time on a television series set, it was an amazing experience for both of us. So much more happening than on a commercial shoot! More people, more activity, different wardrobe, far more excitement. It was sad not to complete the vacation with the rest of the family, but this was not to be missed either!

I juggled my time between taking Kirk and Candace on the never-ending auditions. The more they worked, the more auditions they got calls for. Sometimes Robert would take one while I took the other, and sometimes Patty Rock helped out with the driving.

After Kirk proved himself, he started landing parts in television movies, including *Beyond Witch Mountain*, *The Woman Who Willed a Miracle*, *More Than Murder*, and *Starflight: The Plane That Couldn't Land*. At each one, we learned something new. At each one, we made new friends. And at each one, I made sure to bring baskets of my chocolate chip cookies on wrap day.

In 1983, Kirk got the part of Eric on a new series called *Two Marriages*. The drama got good reviews for the season it ran, and Kirk was nominated for an award for his part in a dramatic role. The cast portrayed two families, one with three kids and one with two, living across the street from each other.

Our own family liked the stability that working on a series brought to the house. There were still auditions to run Kirk to, but

Candace in her first commercial, for Mutual of Omaha.

not as many. He had a daily routine now, something that could be counted on.

Candace was making a name for herself as well. She had been making commercials since she was five, even though she didn't have acting lessons either. In her first, Mutual of Omaha, she had a nonspeaking part and wore her blond hair in braids. In the Aunt Jemima Pancake Syrup commercial, she got to shout, "Great pancakes!" while wearing a sweet little antique linen dress and her hair braided. Her favorites, however, were for the Strawberry Shortcake and Cabbage Patch dolls. She also appeared on commercials promoting Kentucky Fried Chicken, Care Bears, Kool-Aid, Chef Boyardee, and even a commercial for a chain saw!

At the Cabbage Patch audition, Candace knew she'd nailed it the moment the audition was over. The casting director had her look at a Cabbage Patch doll as though she was a real mommy loving a real baby. "I just looked at the doll like he did, Mommy. And I know I did it right."

A few times only a "part" of Candace appeared in the commercial—which she thought was pretty weird. For example, only her hand showed up playing with a doll or figurine.

One of her biggest disappointments came when she thought she'd landed a Jell-O commercial with Bill Cosby. But when we arrived, there was another little girl identical to Candace. Candace was hired as a stand-in for the little girl. So while the hired actress was in school, Candace stood in for her so the cameramen would know the correct lighting and height for their camera angles. I reminded her that even though they weren't principle jobs, these were wonderful experiences for a young actress.

Soon after, she quickly landed multiple guest appearance roles on primetime hits such as *St. Elsewhere, T.J. Hooker, TV's Bloopers and Practical Jokes,* and *Who's the Boss?*

I hit my stride, balancing the schedules of the two actors in our family, while Robert kept the two kids at home in his sights.

Just as we thought Kirk might hold onto his job for another season, a TV show running in the same time slot as *Two Marriages* titled, *Cheers,* edged the series off the air.

During his time on *Two Marriages,* Kirk had an event that became funny years later when we looked back on the irony of it.

The teen heartthrob in 1983 happened to be a great kid named C. Thomas Howell, who played on the show with Kirk. One day, the series shot a scene at an all-girls school. When the scene cut, girls surrounded C. Thomas, waving pens and papers, calling his name and asking for autographs.

Thirteen-year-old Kirk watched this from some distance away. He looked at his teacher and said shyly, "I hope someday I can sign an autograph."

His teacher smiled and nodded, "I'm sure you will, Kirk."

chapter 9

Boarding the Roller-Coaster

As manager, I was so busy that one day blurred into the next. The "exciting life" everyone supposed we led was just "normal" to us. And so, when asked what day changed everything for us, we aren't sure what day that would be. Was it the day Fran took the photos of my kids to Iris? Or was it the day Kirk landed his first commercial? What about the day he auditioned for *Growing Pains*? Or was it the day Candace landed *Full House*?

TV scripts begin in the middle of action, in the middle of a story where it's like someone has tossed up a bowl of popcorn and all the pieces fall where they need to be picked up. In movies, the event that changes everything happens after the viewer has gotten comfortable with the normal lives of the main characters.

We can't pull out an extraordinary situation, point to it, and say that this is the moment that everything changed, because the change in our lives happened so slowly, so imperceptibly. Our changes happened in the midst of our daily lives, as those lives were moving along as they had. Little decisions—like letting Fran take those pictures—felt so insignificant at the time. We didn't know what the future would bring.

A school day in 1985 was like any other audition day for the Cameron family. I sat in the van, waiting for Kirk to emerge from middle school. I knew the moment he saw me, because his shoulders sagged, his head dropped, and he started walking slower. He turned to pause and talk to his friends, ignoring my frantic waving. "Come on, Kirk, we're going to be late."

He either didn't hear me, or didn't want to hear me. He let himself be sidetracked by every kid who came along. Eventually, he dragged himself into the car.

Kirk : I didn't want to go on this audition any more than I wanted to go on other ones. I hated the dorky striped Izod shirt Mom made me wear. Once we were far enough away from school so no one would see me, I tugged on the shoulders of my comfortable T-shirt, pulling it over my head and traded it for the scratchy striped one. I tucked it into my jeans, hating that each shove of the shirt into the jeans made me look even more like a dork. Then I had to put on a belt. Whoa, Mom. You'd think the producers of whatever I was auditioning for would want me to look like a normal teen. Not a kid who looks like some Grandma's idea of the perfect teen. I also didn't want to comb my hair. Didn't know if I would.

We drove the whole way—as usual—in complete conversational silence. I'd long ago given up the idea that we could have mother-son chats during these endless trips "over the hill" into Hollywood and back. Kirk leaned against the door, his eyelids as if they had little weights in them, so heavy that he couldn't hold them up anymore. And then, as usual, he went to sleep.

I turned on the radio and hummed along to some top 40 song. I didn't want to wake Kirk. Looking at the clock, my heart skipped a beat. We were going to be late. If we were late, Iris would find out. And if Iris found out—I'd sure hear about it. "Honey!" she'd say in her loud, rasping voice, "As long as you're with me, you're on time for auditions. Get that? I've got a reputation to keep, and I'm not losing it because you couldn't get your kid there on time."

My stomach roiled. I hated confrontation. I hated to disappoint. And doing both with Iris was the worst.

Still, I had precious cargo in my van, and I needed to drive safely. As is typical in the Los Angeles basin, the traffic is uncertain. We'd be slowed for a few miles to a near standstill, then suddenly the traffic would break, and we were off and running again. It didn't make sense.

As we got off the freeway, Kirk woke. He took his comb out and ran it through his dark curls. "We're late," I said, trying to keep my voice even. I stopped in front of the door of ABC Studios. "Get up there. I'll park and meet you."

Kirk : Once I realized we were late, I took the stairs two at a time. I had received my sides ahead of time, and had given them a quick glance. I didn't pay much attention to them, because this audition was no different than any other. I knew Mom was very nervous about both this audition and the *Lucas* film she hoped I'd get a callback for. And now I was adding to Mom's stress by making us late. I knocked on the studio door. Someone answered. "You're late," he said. He looked at his watch. "Auditions closed at 4:30. It's 5:00."

"Wait." I put my foot out, hoping he wouldn't close the door. "My mom will kill me if I don't do this audition."

He looked over his shoulder, muffled things were said, and then he opened the door. "Okay."

I knew that I'd probably lost the audition. But at least I could tell Mom that they'd let me in. I stood in front of the camera. "My name is Kirk Cameron. I'm fourteen, and I'm represented by Iris Burton."

"Fine. Go ahead."

I read the lines, interacting with someone who was reading a different part, someone I couldn't see in the darkened room. "Thanks," the man said.

"Hey," I asked, "is this a comedy?"

The men in the room burst into laughter. "Yeah, it's a comedy," one said.

Later I learned one said to another, "He's not the sharpest knife in the drawer, but he sounds like Mike."

Kirk : Mom flew into the waiting room as I entered it from the opposite end, her blond hair falling out of whatever she kept it held back in. Her face was, as usual after an audition, excited, open, eager for news.

"Well?" I asked. "How did it go?" I tried not to sound too enthusiastic. I knew that made the kids clam up. But I couldn't help it.

Kirk shrugged. "They laughed."

"Is that a good thing?"

Kirk shrugged again, heading for the exit door.

I smiled and followed him. "What did they say? Did they like you? Do you think you got the part?" I knew Kirk would have a sense about this. After enough auditions, the kids get to know whether or not they did well. They can tell by how the producers and director release them.

Kirk opened the door and kept going, pausing long enough for me to catch the heavy door. "Do you think you'll get a callback?" I don't know why I kept asking questions. I knew Kirk wouldn't answer. Neither of the kids did. They liked to keep their auditions to themselves. Sometimes they'd let a tiny bit of information leak out, but mostly it was all body language. Today I couldn't read Kirk's. It was somewhere between, "I have a chance," and, "I feel stupid."

I unlocked the door of our van, and slid into the seat. Kirk got in, took off his belt, and switched back to his comfortable T-shirt.

"Do you have homework tonight?"

Kirk shrugged.

I took a deep breath and tried not to let his distant attitude hurt me. I needed to remember this was just Kirk. He was quiet. After school, after shooting a commercial, Kirk just wanted to hide out in his room. He liked to play his guitar and just relax alone.

"Do you want to get something from McDonalds?"

Kirk stared out the window at the rush-hour traffic. It took him a moment to answer. "Okay."

When we got home, there was a message on the answering machine from Iris. "Kirk's got another callback, honey. For that feature film, *Lucas*. This is looking good. Be there at four on Thursday."

Click.

I ran out of the bedroom closet where I kept the machine. "Kirk! You have a callback for *Lucas*!"

Bridgette looked at him from stirring the cooking ground turkey. "What's this, the third one?"

Kirk thought a moment. "Yeah."

"What's the movie about?"

"It's about some nerdy kid—"

"That's you," Melissa said, setting the plates on the table.

"Shut up," Kirk replied.

"And?" Bridgette asked.

"This nerdy kid," he glared at Melissa, daring her to say something, "tries to stand up to the bullies at school so the other kids will accept him. He's also trying to get on the football team. And there's a girl in there somewhere."

"So why would they want you?" Bridgette asked.

"He's the perfect nerd," Melissa said.

Kirk took a kitchen towel and snapped it at her. "And *that*, my dear sister," he said sarcastically, "is in the movie. So I need to practice snapping towels."

Melissa shrieked and took off running, the napkins for dinner still in her hand. Kirk didn't bother chasing her. He kicked back on the bench seat behind the kitchen table.

Kirk not only survived the *Lucas* callback, but the studio told us, "Pack your bags, Mrs. Cameron! Kirk is our number one choice. This will be a three-month shooting commitment, so do what you need to do to get your family in order. We do want Kirk to come in for a screen test. We want to nerd him up a little to see what we'll need to do for the film."

As excited as I was, I wondered whether or not that little series thing would come through.

Lord, which one? I prayed. A feature sure sounded good, but a series would last longer. As Kirk's manager, I needed to help guide him. As a mother, I felt a lot of pressure to not say anything that would push him to do something he didn't want or wasn't ready for. The stress was so great that I just prayed, "Your will, Lord, not mine."

I began to believe that *Lucas* was our answer. We hadn't heard from ABC about their series, so I not only packed our bags as we were told, but I also attended the necessary details and preparations for the family while we were gone.

While we were at the studio, preparing for the screen test, we were quite surprised to see a young boy named Cory Haim come into the audition. He had just finished working in Arizona on a film, and they were setting him up to do a screen test also. It was upsetting to know we weren't the only choice, when we were led to believe we were, and had gone to all the trouble of making family preparations.

I was very disappointed and somewhat angry. But I walked to the back of the studio and prayed one of my little, casual prayers—casual in how it was said, but certainly not in how I felt. *God. I'm upset, but I want You to take care of this. Whatever happens, I'll trust You.*

After the screen test, we went home and got the call we sort of expected—that Kirk did not get the part in *Lucas.*

Even though I'd kind of tossed the whole thing at God, I can't say that I wasn't very disappointed. After seeing Kirk, Candace, and Melissa on commercials, and then Kirk on a series, I really wanted to see one of my kids on the big screen. I thought that would be so cool! And I guess I thought *Lucas* would be it.

For anyone who thinks this business is just one fun event after another, they're mistaken. Instead, it's a real emotional roller-coaster ride! One minute you're up, and the next, you're down. There are promises made, and then broken. There's hope given, and hopes dashed.

I tried to teach the kids that the most important thing in this business is for them to do the best they could and then have fun! If it stopped being fun, then they didn't have to do it anymore. Yet, they never indicated to me that they were disappointed or wanted to quit. Sure, auditions could be tedious, but the rest of it was worth the auditions.

The kids handled these roller coaster situations pretty well. I didn't do as well as they did. I took the downturns a little harder. I had to learn that I couldn't show my emotions during the disappointing times. If I did, they would pick up on it and think they had done something wrong or that they had disappointed me.

A few days after *Lucas* took us on the roller coaster to the bottom, we got a phone call from Iris that ABC had called. "Honey, this is another callback. They want Kirk to audition with a family unit in front of the producers for the television series."

Our roller-coast flew up again.

chapter 10

Growing Pains

I sat in the near-empty casting director's office, trying to read my book. The producer's callback for the television series could last some time as they had the entire family unit audition together. Did the family unit connect? Did they visually look like a family? Did they interact like a family?

God, I prayed while staring at blurred words on the pages of my book, *it would be so cool if Kirk got this part. It would be so cool for him to be on another series. It's so much easier than auditioning for commercials all the time. It's better for our family. And it would be so much fun for Kirk. If it's okay with You ..."*

I looked up from the book at the two other mothers who sat there, also trying to pass the time. Their body language, probably like mine, showed they were nervous. A crossed leg bouncing. Twisting a wedding ring. A finger resting against mouth, not quite being nibbled. Shifting in seats. We had already introduced ourselves. We weren't in competition with each other. If the producers chose this family unit, all three of our kids would be in—at least for the pilot.

Although being on a series held the promise of stability, no one was ever secure. If it didn't work for whatever reason, even mid-season a character can be replaced.

I looked at my book again. Another prayer floating gently through my mind. *Please God? Please?*

Another family unit had auditioned earlier. Had the producers already made up their minds and were just holding to their obligations? Or were Kirk and his family unit getting a fair chance?

I wished I could plaster my ear at the door. Once in a while I could hear laughter. A good sign, for sure. But not knowing if the other family unit had also brought laughter, how could I judge?

Sometimes we mothers would look up and give each other rueful smiles. We'd spent the first fifteen minutes chatting about what all stage mothers have in common: kids and business.

"What products has your child represented?"

"Any movies? Series?"

"Who has he worked with?"

The conversation dwindled a little, and then vanished, nerves and desire to hear whatever we could through that solid door silencing us.

Kirk burst through the door first. "Okay, Mom. Let's go."

All three mothers looked at his face for some sign, some indication ...

"Mom," Kirk insisted. "Let's go."

I came to my senses, closed the book, and grabbed my purse. I stuffed the book inside it as I smiled to the other mothers. "Goodbye," I said. "Good luck."

Once in the van, I put the keys in the ignition. "Well?" I asked, trying to sound like it didn't really matter. "How did it go? What do you think?"

"It was fun."

I tried not to show surprise that I actually got some reaction out of him. "Do you have a chance?"

Kirk shrugged. "I guess." Then he assumed "the position." Leaning his head against the window, he closed his eyes and fell asleep.

We hadn't been home long when the phone rang. Sometimes I got jumpy when I waited for a call to give us the outcome of an event. But this call was too soon, so I didn't think it would have anything to do with the day's events.

"Congratulations," Iris rasped.

I mentally sorted through which auditions Candace had been on, and what we might be expecting an answer for. Nothing.

"They want Kirk for *Growing Pains*."

"What?"

Iris laughed. "I guess they know what they want, and Kirk's family unit is it."

I sat back in a chair.

"I'll be in negotiations. Anything you want?"

I couldn't think. "A good teacher, I guess."

"Anyone in particular?"

I couldn't think of anyone. We'd had so many. And Kirk's teacher on *Two Marriages* had been fine. I didn't feel like being particular. "No, I guess not."

"Anything else?"

I wouldn't have known what to ask for anyway. I was grateful for whatever Iris had negotiated in the past. "Whatever you think is best."

"We'll be in touch."

Click.

I closed my eyes and smiled, holding my arms around myself. I could barely hope that this series might stick. *Thank you, God*, I whispered.

"KIRK!" I shouted. "You got it! You got the series! Wahoo!"

Kirk stuck his head outside his bedroom door and shouted, "Really? Cool." Then I heard the door click shut.

I wanted to crank up the jukebox and dance. Why did my kids just take all this in stride? A new series is such an exciting prospect. If it hits the right time slot and the right buttons, they can go on for six, seven, eight years. A steady job is the goal of most actors, and here, for us, it was on the horizon. We may not have gotten the *Lucas* movie, but a series is steady work.

I announced the news at the dinner table, although everyone pretty much already knew.

Robert looked at Kirk, "You know, Kirk you're still …"

"… going to go to college," the kids all said in bored unison.

"Just so you know," Robert reminded them. "You can't go anywhere without …"

"… a college education," the kids chorused, then fell into laughter.

Later that night, when we were alone, I said, "Robert, why can't you be happy for the kids when they book?"

"I am happy. It's just that this is all a fantasy, Barbara. It's not real. It won't last. Even Iris says over and over how they'd better have something else going in their lives."

"But can't you let them enjoy it now?"

"Sure. I admit they're making a little money they can use to pay for college. That's nice."

I went to sleep with the usual sadness that spread from my heart and lay heavy in my stomach. Why couldn't Robert understand? Why couldn't he enjoy this with us?

In the morning, I thanked God again. I wondered if my family knew about this secret relationship I had with God. Inside, I was still the little girl who didn't want to go to hell. I wanted to be good enough and do things right. It seemed like I must be okay, because life was mostly good. Inside, I felt so empty, but really, did I have anything to complain about? I had a house, great kids, a husband who worked and provided, and a little hobby job I found fun.

I kept my belief about God a secret. Sure, I put out the nativity scene every Christmas. I told the kids that the true Christmas was about the birth of baby Jesus. Kirk had rolled his eyes the last Christmas and said, "Yeah, whatever, Mom."

And one day, while driving home from an audition with a gorgeous sunset coloring the sky, I said something to Candace about God creating the beauty around us, and she looked at me like I'd just said I believed in aliens.

If I even tried to have a discussion about serious issues that might be facing the kids and what I felt about them, they'd all say something similar: "Come on, Mom. No one thinks like that anymore."

Only once did I blurt out something forceful about God. Kirk had come home from school and threw open the refrigerator. After examining the contents and finding them totally insufficient, he muttered, "G— d— it."

I lit into him. "Kirk, don't you *ever* disrespect God like that again. Do you hear me?"

"Come on Mom, there's no such thing as God!"

I couldn't believe my son said that. I felt so incredibly sad and angry at the same time. "There IS and you WILL respect Him and not take His name in vain."

He looked stunned. "Yes, Mom."

I guess I shocked the occasional fight right out of him. His shoulders slumped, and he slunk away.

So I kept my thoughts about God and my prayers to Him a secret. I didn't really know if I was even praying right. I didn't know what

God thought of me, but I guessed that I was good enough. Certainly, our lives were going well.

Growing Pains didn't take off like a flash as the studios had hoped. The girl originally chosen for Carol Seaver, Kirk's on-screen sister, didn't work out, and a new one—Tracey Gold—took her place. The family gelled and enjoyed working with each other. They teased and joked with each other, becoming great friends along the way.

I loved sitting on the set and watching him act. I couldn't get enough of seeing my boy do amazing things. He came alive in front of a camera, interacting with it in such a way that even the cameramen remarked, "He has something going with the camera." If you could say someone flirted with a camera, Kirk did.

I couldn't believe how fast he could remember not only his lines, but where he was supposed to stand, what object he was told to pick up, and what he was supposed to do with it once it was in his hand. And he did it all seamlessly. I think I could have done one or the other, but not everything at once!

In time, Robert and I both had our chances to try out what our kids did so well. Each of us was asked to be on one of the shows and have a very short, very easy line.

They asked Robert to play Kirk twenty years in the future. Robert agreed to do it as long as he didn't have to say any lines. "That's fine," the director said.

But when the script came out, the writers had generously given him a whole paragraph to memorize! Robert tried every trick in the book to get those words memorized. He couldn't do it. He went to a top acting coach, Howard Fine, for help. After an hour, Howard said, "I think this is as good as you're going to get."

When Robert sat on his assigned stool on the set, he couldn't say the simplest lines. He froze.

I'm sure it didn't help that the producers and directors—and the entire cast—who all liked Robert by now, stood around the monitors laughing and whooping it up. Robert had given them all a hard time in his playful, direct way, and now they were getting back at him. Joey Scott, the producer for the show, said, "As bad as Robert says he did, he did far worse than that. The moment we heard the command, 'Roll!', all movement from Robert stopped."

Eventually, instead of having Robert say something Mike Seaver would have said, they had Kirk mimic some of Robert's mannerisms so it looked like Robert was acting—when it was really Kirk doing all the work.

The director of *Growing Pains* asked me to be on an episode as well. I thought it would be fine. I only had to stand in one place, let Kirk—who happened to be on the floor—slowly look up at my face, realize he just pleaded his love to the wrong woman, and say, "Break a leg," I, too, froze. The only scene Robert and I managed to play with ease and without freezing was later on *Full House* when we got to play a couple making out in the park. No problem there!

Life took on a steady rhythm with Kirk on the series. Robert's reveille woke the school kids in the morning. They had to be eating breakfast by 6:30 or they didn't get breakfast. Each of the girls and Robert took turns making the meal. At promptly 7:05, Robert's little red VW truck took off for school taxi service. Shortly after that, Kirk and I got in my van, and we drove to the ABC Studios where Kirk immediately started school. On Mondays, he'd be pulled out for the first script read-through, where the entire cast read the script for the week. During the read-through, the producers, directors, and writers gathered together to smooth out the rough places they'd discovered as the actors read. The actors could also make comments about the script. Kirk went back to school while the actors began to walk through the marks and directions for that particular story. Kirk and the other child actors had stand-ins, who played them while school was in session. The stand-in needed to take excellent notes and be able to convey this information to the children so the child actors would know what was expected of them when they returned to the set.

This, too, amazed me—how Kirk could pick up precisely what was expected of him by listening to the stand-in.

After finishing three hours of schooling required by California law, the child actors were free to again become part of rehearsal.

I quickly learned that the actors were not supposed to memorize the words verbatim, but were to know the material thoroughly. The writers often made changes throughout the week, and everyone needed to be flexible and to adjust quickly to those changes in script. Understanding the material, the actors could then grasp the concepts and which words needed to be exact and which didn't.

Tuesdays and Wednesdays, school came first, then rehearsals. Thursdays were block and tape days—kind of a camera rehearsal where the cast did everything as rehearsed, in the exact spots where they were supposed to be. The show was taped to be certain they had a perfect show "in the can."

Fridays the live audience came in and got to watch the show being taped again. If the crew shot a better scene, they used the live scene. If not, they could always revert to the one in the can.

The live audience gave the actors new energy. Listening to an audience laugh at the right moment sent thrills up my spine. I can't imagine how much more it did for the actors.

On Thursdays and Fridays, the kids had to be extra flexible, because their schooling could come in twenty-minute shots between shooting their scenes.

When Kirk wasn't rehearsing one of his scenes, I loved to go from trailer to trailer, talking with whoever was available. Cameramen, grips, any of the crew who weren't tied up at the moment became

Barb and Candace on the set of Full House. *Barb just had her makeup done for her first appearance as one of the moms in an episode called "Joey's Place."*

people to converse with. The mothers of the actors, Sonja (Jeremy Miller), Bonnie (Tracey Gold), and I all sat together cackling and talking like the mother hens we were. We talked about our marriages, our children, the industry—life. Bonnie always put us to shame with her extravagant, generous parties. Stepping into her home at Christmas, you'd think you'd stepped into a high-class department store decked out with every beautiful decoration imaginable.

At home, Robert picked up Bridgette, Melissa, and Candace every day after school, brought them home, and set them down at the kitchen table to do homework. As long as the girls did their homework, didn't watch television when they weren't supposed to (Robert felt the TV if he'd been out on an errand to be sure they hadn't been watching), and followed his other many rules—life was good. The problem was, Bridgette couldn't keep up with the program. She tried so hard to do her homework, but couldn't grasp some of the concepts. Robert, tired of dealing with stubborn kids all day at school, certainly wasn't going to take the same behavior from his own child at home. I hated coming home to a crying child so many days, and tried to lighten up the situation and make Bridgette feel like she wasn't stupid.

As the days, weeks, months of filming passed, sadness and distance grew and blossomed within me.

chapter 11

Making a Wish

Many days, Candace had auditions. If so, it necessitated a one-hour drive from the studio (leaving Kirk in the capable hands of one of the other mothers) to pick up Candace from school, another hour drive to take her to the audition, and a ninety-minute drive in traffic back home after waiting for Kirk to finish work for the day.

All that driving allowed plenty of time for me to think. Always being a positive person, I continually ran Robert's good qualities on my mental screen. He took half the load, he loved the kids and me, he worked hard, he never complained about the long hours Kirk, Candace, and I were gone. We had a great time on beach Sundays. Others respected him and came to him for advice.

What the mind says and what the heart feels are sometimes two separate things, waging an uncomfortable battle within. No matter how hard I tried to see Robert's good qualities, my heart felt shriveled up and dying. Was it wrong to want to be loved? Was it wrong to expect my husband to not only say he loved me, but to show it by speaking kindly to me? Was my desire to be *one* foolish?

I loved the set. I craved being on the set. Not only was it fun—much more fun than being a housewife—once there, I had status and value. I was Barbara Cameron, Kirk's mom. I was the cookie lady who brought an enormous basket of my chocolate chip cookies every tape day. I was the lady who sat in the corner with the mothers of the extras and talked with them—mothers who were usually ostracized from the mother's clique merely by the fact that our little group of mothers of the cast and reoccurring characters knew each other well.

Friday nights I got dressed up, gathered my girls, and we all went to tape night—sometimes without Robert. Robert usually had some project going and wanted to keep working on it. You couldn't keep me away from tape night.

The girls loved it, too. When they entered the set, everyone greeted them like they belonged, too. The audience whispered, and you could hear the girls' names. And the girls loved watching their brother act. I never tired of watching him, of hearing the audience respond to him. I also played sort of "mother" to the audience. If I saw someone who looked like they might be too hot, I got a bottle of water to them. I greeted those around me. I felt that if these people went to this much trouble to come see the show, I wanted to help them enjoy it.

The family thought it was fun that the writers incorporated things that happened in our own family into the show. For example, in one of the first shows, Carol got the other kids to picket Mom for unfair treatment of mice.

Each week, the writers engaged Kirk in conversations, trying to find out what happened in his own family. Kirk loves to tell stories, and tells them well, keeping everyone laughing.

Along with the show, my life took off. I loved being Manager Mom. Auditions for Candace still lacked the element of *fun*, but sometimes we'd see Emily Schulman, a girl Candace had worked with in commercials. The girls would chatter in the corner, playing the lines off each other, while I talked with Emily's mom. The jealousy and visual backstabbing that went on so often in the casting directors' offices melted away when the Schulmans were there.

I told Candace what I had told Kirk, that this should always be fun and it didn't matter whether she got the job or not. And I meant it. I really didn't care if she got the job. I cared far more that this was fun for her.

Sometimes, when Candace didn't get the job, she'd feel bad. "Did I not do a good enough job, Mom?"

I'd sit down and put her in my lap. "You know, Candace, they might have been looking for something else. Like different color hair, or eyes, or personality. Maybe they wanted someone more nerdy, or someone drop-dead gorgeous."

"I did my best, Mom, I really did."

I hugged her tight, and then looked her right in the eyes. "Then that's the most important thing, isn't it? You did your best, and that's great. I'm proud of you."

"You are? But I didn't get the job."

"I'm proud of you whether you get the job or not. I'm proud of my girl when she does her best and comes out having had fun." I lifted her chin and said, "Do you have fun acting?"

Candace nodded her head, her eyes lighting up. "I love to act."

"Then let's keep you acting."

I didn't mind being so busy. I, the former fearful Los Angeles freeway driver, became confident. I knew my way around and knew how long it took to get almost anywhere.

The only thing I couldn't do was drive to the hotel where Emily Schulman lived. I drove a van with a stick shift, and that hill where the hotel perched scared me to death.

"Please, Mommy," Candace would beg. "Can't we go visit Emily?"

I felt so bad that I had to tell her no. "I can't drive on that hill, honey. I don't want to take any chances that we could roll back down the hill and get into an accident. It's not worth it."

As often happens when you love your kids, Candace wore me down. After many pleas and many disappointments, I agreed to try. "Your dad taught me a little trick, and I'll see if it works."

I drove up the hill to the stop sign. At the sign, I pulled on the emergency brake. When I started to move again, I pushed the gas, let up a little on the clutch, then quickly took off the emergency brake. And it worked! I'd achieved another breakthrough of my fears.

In addition, talking with Iris no longer tied my stomach in knots. I achieved what I'd set out to do—get Iris to respect me as a mom/manager. She didn't need to yell at me. I did everything as I should—and was a stellar example.

Iris called me one day. "Listen, honey, I need surgery."

"I'm so sorry, Iris. Are you going to be okay? Is there anything I can do?"

"Yeah, yeah, I'll be okay." I could see her waving her hand as though I stood right in front of her, cigarette smoke trailing in the air behind her fingers cradling the cigarette. "But my assistant took off last week. Following her heart or some damn thing. I don't have anyone to answer the phones. I can't leave the business for a day."

"You want me to come in, Iris?"

"Wouldja, honey? All you have to do is answer the phones."

"I can do that."

"And send people out on auditions and read the faxed *Breakdowns* and call kids to send them on auditions. The messenger service will pick up the photos and bios."

I swallowed back insecurity. Would I mess things up so much that I'd fall out of grace with Iris? "Of course, I'll do it."

I actually enjoyed those days of working in her office. Calling up mothers to alert them to auditions and callbacks, and hearing the checked excitement in their voices made all the nervousness worth it.

And Iris couldn't have been more appreciative. The more I interacted with her, the more I saw how her rough exterior was like the crust on crème brûlée. She looked hard, but underneath she was warm, sweet, and wonderful.

Kirk couldn't help but be a lot like Mike Seaver, and Mike Seaver was a lot like Kirk. As Kirk loves to say, "And I look a lot like Mike, too!"

The writers wrote to Kirk's strengths and to his personality, while also drawing out of him things that he wasn't. For example, Kirk, unlike Mike, is anything but dumb. But Kirk also has that sweet, innocent smile that can win over anyone without saying a word. That smile could cover more bad behavior!

So when he convinced the grips to help him play a joke on the directors and producers, he just smiled. And when the directors and producers couldn't find their chairs after a break, Kirk just smiled, never looking up toward the rafters where all the chairs hung, swinging gently in the shifting air.

Or when he set off little cans of sulfur underneath the bleachers. That awful smell lingered throughout the entire set for hours.

On one occasion, Kirk knew a coworker had put his car keys in his pants in the wardrobe room, so he snuck the keys and hijacked the guy's car. That little trickster drove the car over to the "Fantasy Island" lot and put all kinds of vegetation—bushes, banana leaves, whatever he could find—on the car to hide it. After the show was over, when the guy discovered his car wasn't where he left it. He spent hours looking all over the lot until he found where Kirk had hidden it.

Soon the crew nicknamed him "devil boy." But that didn't stop him. Kirk continued to play practical jokes on everyone. He'd sneak more keys from pockets, hide the cars all over the Warner Brothers lot, and then get a fall guy to send a note to the person that someone was seen taking their car from the lot.

He switched the cables on the cameras on tape night while the camera operators were having dinner. When it came time to tape the show, the operators suddenly realized they had to use the zoom to focus, and focus to zoom if they were to get the shots right.

Kirk had an odd way of handling the need to have high energy on *Growing Pains*. If he didn't have a scene to work on, he might be in school, or giving the crew a bad time, or talking with the other cast members (or playing more practical jokes). If he had a scene coming up, I could see him sitting in his chair, looking for all the world like the most depressed kid you've ever seen. He seemed to have vacated his body. His hands were tucked under his chin, holding it up. His eyes were either closed or staring vacantly at the floor. He slouched, looking quite small. At first, the crew would ask, "Is he okay?"

"I don't know," I would answer, a bit baffled myself.

It didn't take long for us to notice that the moment the director called, "ROLL!" Kirk was out of that chair and *ON*. He came up to speed so fast, you'd think someone had stuck a pin in his backside. When the director called, "CUT!" Kirk resumed his depressed-looking position. We all later figured that's how Kirk conserved energy and surrounded himself with the necessary "alone space" he needed as an introvert. (Later, we'd see Candace use the same trick.)

After a full day's work, Kirk and I would crawl into the van and head home. Kirk usually slept, and I listened to the radio. At home, someone had usually made those turkey tacos, or we'd pick up McDonald's for everyone on the way. When dinner was over, Kirk preferred to retreat in his room.

Tape night, however, was party night. On Friday nights our energy flew and we laughed and talked all the way home. If we had friends who had come to the taping, we'd invite them to a restaurant where we would go to unwind. Sometimes the taping could last until very late—11:00—and then we'd all just go home and crash.

The roles for Candace picked up. She had guest parts in television series and TV movies. She also took part in a *TV's Bloopers and Practical Jokes*, playing the part of a bratty kid to play a joke on Cindy Lauper. Candace adored Cindy at that time. Cindy had just recorded her hit, "Girls Just Wanna Have Fun," and Candace loved the song. In the joke, Candace and another little boy acted as siblings whom Cindy needed to baby-sit while a friend of hers had a fake interview. Candace and the boy pretended to be great little kids until the other adults had left for their "meeting." They acted like total brats, being rude to Cindy, who wanted to be gracious even though these kids were being so awful. After the practical joke had been played, Cindy very kindly gave Candace the lightning bolt hairclip she'd been wearing. Candace treasured that little gift for a long time.

We rejoiced when ABC renewed *Growing Pains* for another season. During the initial run of the first season, the show didn't do very well, and we were all certain it would be canceled. While in summer reruns though, the show suddenly took off, and everyone knew it was going to be a hit. I didn't know until later that the producers immediately recognized that this show, originally with a different purpose in mind, had become Kirk's show, and the fans multiplied like little bunnies. They loved Mike Seaver and developed an insatiable desire to know more about him, to be more like him, to be close to him.

Once the show shot off like a rocket, the Make-A-Wish and Starlight Foundations began to get a flood of wishes from kids to meet Mike Seaver. Soon he was the number one requested person to meet. So every Friday night for the rest of the popularity of *Growing Pains*, a very ill or terminal child sat in the audience, eager to meet Mike Seaver.

Producer, Joey Scott, Kirk, and I took this as a very serious assignment. We knew from the foundations that most of these kids would not get a chance to grow to adulthood. The tape nights were booked up so far in advance that it might take a child six to eight months to visit the show and meet Kirk. During those months of waiting, the anticipation of their dream coming true helped them rally

Sometimes the Camerons would invite special guests home for dinner. Here's Candace with Amanda, one of the Make-A-Wish children.

and grow stronger. Many of these kids actually got better during their wait. But once they achieved their wish, with nothing else to keep them going, they could deteriorate rapidly and die soon after.

With such knowledge, how could we do anything less than our best? How could we just say hello and let it go with a handshake and a smile? My heart reached out to these children and their families. I had four healthy, happy children. Bridgette had been very sick as a little girl, and I had feared for her. But her uncle had bought her a special scooter to develop her endurance. I had seen what love and help could do, and I wanted to give this to these struggling, hurting families.

We found people to donate services, and some we just made happen on our own. We tried to find out from Make-A-Wish and Starlight everything we could about these families. We wanted all to feel special and in the limelight—for something other than the illness.

Kirk with another Make-A-Wish friend, Melanie Brown.

For too long, these kids had been seen as *special* because they were sick. Now we wanted them to feel special just for being themselves— without the illness. And we wanted to include the entire family in whatever we did.

We learned that in these families, every emotional moment, every dollar, every ounce of energy went to these kids. There was no time or money for the parents to spend on each other. The siblings often felt left out since so much attention went to caring for the health of their brother or sister. This wish became something important to give a gift to the entire family, to make it special for all of them. If we could lift the load off these parents for any time whatsoever, that's what we would strive to do.

For some, we had a limousine pick them up from their hotel to bring them to the show. Once there, we treated them like royalty. Part of our goal was to have the others in the audience wonder who these special people were, to get them whispering, their curiosity growing. The first surprise of the night often got our producer, Joey Scott, in trouble. But he stayed strong and helped make it happen. In the middle of a scene, Kirk would stop the taping and say something like, "Tonight we have a very special person in the audience. This person means a lot to me." He'd continue whetting the appetite of the audience. And then he would announce the child's name. On a number of occasions, Kirk would go to a closet on the set, and instead of pulling out an actor's coat, he would remove an official *Growing Pains* jacket, embroidered with the child's name, and hand it to the child.

Some were given scripts signed by the cast. I would ask production if we could get some T-shirts and hats with the name of the show and give them to the kids. We'd be sure they met the cast, had photos taken with the cast—on the set if possible—and got all the autographs they wanted. They'd have a special time with Kirk alone—for photos and just visiting.

It wasn't much, but to these kids it was more than what they expected or experienced if they'd visited other shows. I would be their hostess for the evening and do whatever I could to make their experience an enjoyable one. If it was possible, sometimes we would do something special, like meet them at their hotel and take them to breakfast or lunch. After the show, if the family wanted, we'd stay and talk for hours. Kirk, with his friendly, easy-going personality, could get them all laughing and feeling as though they were the most important people in the world. Nothing was more important than our times with these families.

One Christmas, we decided to give an extra Christmas present to a visiting child, taking over the details ourselves. We sent a limo to pick up the family at the airport. The driver, dressed as Santa Claus, waited for his very important passenger in the airport holding a sign with the little girl's name on it. Joey and I bought a huge, life-sized, stuffed animal that was waiting in the back seat of the limo. The fluffy white bear held a note from Kirk telling the little girl that he couldn't wait for her to arrive.

She came to the show and had a great time. We did the usual, then said our good-byes. Then, as an added surprise, we had the cast and some of the crew waiting for the family at a really fun restaurant with a cake, balloons, and a sign—a party ready to happen. We arrived before the family to set up. Everyone in the place was waiting to see what very important person we were all there to celebrate. The little girl beamed, her face shining, the rest of the family astounded at this gift.

After our little party, we said good-bye again, which is always very hard on the children.

But the next morning, Kirk and Joey were waiting for this little girl in the lobby of the hotel. She was very sad to have to say good-bye to Kirk again. Instead, they swept her off to a surprise visit to Disneyland.

Many times, we didn't want these times to end. The good-byes were difficult. We'd connected with these kids quickly. And to know that most of them would not survive their illness made the good-byes even more difficult. So we'd invite them to our home for dinner. Our whole family welcomed them, and we had great impromptu parties. Robert and Kirk could keep everyone laughing. The girls simply swept everyone inside as though these were their new best friends. Sometimes, the families didn't really have more plans for the weekend. We'd invite them to Candace's cabin in Big Bear, or to go to the beach. Anything to keep that joy and life going.

And we saw small miracles. Maybe they weren't lasting, but they gave the families a deep, profound sense of gratitude for the experience. One woman told us that her daughter, who had been on a respirator as well as a feeding tube, got so caught up in the excitement and joy of the evening, that she felt "normal." She asked for something to eat, telling her mom she was hungry. "She hasn't said that in a very long time," the mom told us, tears streaming down her face.

These children were Kirk's favorite fans, and became an important part of his future. Somehow life had blessed us beyond our wildest dreams, and it seemed only fair and natural to share those blessings with anyone who would need them. And as far as we knew, no one needed blessings more than these.

chapter 12

Full House

In 1987, which was two years after Kirk began *Growing Pains*, Candace went on an audition for a television series. She disappeared into the audition room and when she came out, she was crying. "Mom, I got the callback."

"Then what's wrong?"

"The casting director called the producers before she let me go and told them that I was *okay*. Not *good*, just *okay*. I could do better, Mom."

So I knocked on the casting director's door. "Do you have a minute?" I asked. "Candace would like a chance to redo her audition."

"I told her she was going to be called back. She'll be hearing from her agent."

I gave her a fake smile. "It would be really nice if you told Candace exactly what you want and let her do it. She's very good at taking direction."

The casting director seemed to think only for a moment. "All right."

Candace disappeared again, then reappeared grinning from ear to ear. "She said I did *great*."

Candace always wanted to do her best, and knew that she could do even better when the casting director told her clearly what they wanted. When she auditioned for the Cabbage Patch commercial, she knew what to do, because the director modeled it for her. When she left the room, she had known she had done exactly what he asked, and knew she'd have the part.

At the same time she auditioned for the series, she had also auditioned for a film titled *Punchline*, starring Sally Field and Tom Hanks. I held my breath through the first audition, then the callback. *God*, I had prayed long ago, *I would really love to have one of my kids be able to act with Tom Hanks or Sally Field.* And now here was her chance to do both at once!

I can't lie and say it didn't matter to me. It did! I didn't want it to matter, but I was so excited about the possibility. And then she got the part! I did so many happy dances with Candace.

It turned out that Candace's role was to play the daughter of Sally Field and her on-film husband, John Goodman. Candace didn't get to play any face-to-face scenes with Tom Hanks, although she did have a scene where she talked on the phone with him, and it delighted her that he was really on the other end.

I met Sally Field, but I'm sure she wasn't interested in meeting another actress's mom! She'd met so many in her day. It was still a thrill for me, and I enjoyed watching Candace be able to interact with her on the set. Sally was very nice to Candace. When Candace turned ten during the filming of the movie, she couldn't believe it when she found a large birthday gift basket in her dressing room from Sally.

As a memento of the great time she had making this movie, Candace collected tape that was used as marks for the actors to stand in the proper position on the sets and rolled it into a seven-inch diameter ball. Then she had much of the cast and crew sign it.

During the filming, we received news that Candace had done a great job at her producer's audition and had been accepted for the part of DJ Tanner on the new series, *Full House*. The only problem was that the filming for the pilot conflicted with Candace completing her obligations on *Punchline*. Iris stepped in and made some calls, discovering that the producers of *Full House* liked Candace so well, they were willing to adjust their filming schedule to accommodate her. Jeff Franklin, the show's creator and show runner says, "Candace was exceptional. We had her read for the part and she nailed it. After her audition we said, 'Well, we're done with that role.' She was completely real. It's very unusual for a child actress to be that comfortable in her skin and at ease with the whole process."

When we arrived at the Sony studios in Culver City to film the pilot, we were ushered into greatness. *The Wizard of Oz* had been filmed on that soundstage. The crew told us there was still some yellow of the brick road underneath the layers of flooring. Perhaps the magic of that film hung around a little, infusing the new series with a touch of Glenda's wand. I sure felt like our lives were taking on a magical quality. The little "after-school hobbies" had now grown into full-blown jobs for my young children. Our lives took on a pattern that would dictate our lives for the next eight years.

Soon after Candace began acting on *Full House*, Kirk got his driver's license and bought a new, white Honda Prelude with his earnings to get himself to the *Growing Pains* set and home again. That freed me to be able to concentrate on managing Candace, while still visiting the *Growing Pains* set as well. I didn't stop managing Kirk, as there was always work to do. However, since the show was so well established, I could stop in for business when I needed to, and when I just wanted to connect with friends. And with one person in particular ...

On the sets, I had time to observe the different casts and crews and their personalities. I had the perfect vantage point for watching how they interacted, how they treated others, how they conducted themselves. And on two days a week when additional crew came, one man stood out from the rest. It didn't take long to learn someone's name on the set. People called to each other, and by paying attention, I soon learned his name was Steve. He clowned around with Kirk, playing practical jokes to get back at him. He could banter verbally with the rest of the crew. Everyone seemed to like him. He was fun, clever, kind, and very laid back.

I was not looking for someone to fill the spot that belonged to Robert. I didn't even notice that I had begun to look forward to blocking day more than any other. A tiny seed planted itself in my heart, and I didn't realize I had put it there. Not for a long time.

Everything I'd done for Kirk on *Growing Pains*, I now did for Candace on *Full House*. I worked with the producer to be sure Candace had what she needed. Just like on *Growing Pains*, the cast moms immediately became friends: Jarnie Olsen (Mary-Kate and

Ashley/Michelle), Janice Sweetin (Jodie/Stephanie), and Shari Barber (Andrea/Kimmy Gibbler). We, too, talked about kids, marriages, life, everything, nothing. Occasionally we'd spend time away from the set just being regular women together. Once we even played the parts of moms on *Full House*, dropping off our kids for daycare on a day when Joey was being a housefather.

And just like on *Growing Pains*, the cast took my daughter under their wings and she became a part of a new family. She loved interacting with her "dad" and "uncles" on the show, Bob Saget, John Stamos, and Dave Coulier. They teased her, and she teased them right back. There was a lot of laughter and affection on the set, which I think spread to the viewers as it became one of the most beloved sitcoms ever.

At first, Candace hung out with Andrea and Jodie on the set, and the three would sometimes go into the room where the twins stayed to play with them. She also adored Bob Saget, and the two of them immediately became great pals. I think they appreciated each other's sense of humor. Not only that, Bob appreciated Candace as an actress and as a human being. "The first thing I noticed when I met her is that she was incredibly smart. She was a very talented actress because she had an honesty about her. She didn't play things for the laugh that much; she played things in the sincerity of the moment. The stuff was always very much like what a real person would do in the situation—not over-the-top.

"This is the other thing that really impressed me about Candace— she loved acting. She really, really loved it. When she had a scene, she got really excited to do it. I think in some ways it was not taken for granted, but it was assumed, 'We'll give that to Candace because she'll nail that. It's not going to be a problem with that scene.' (All of the kids were like that. Jodie Sweetin was spot-on, too.) Candace rarely messed up—the only time she did is when she was exhausted, which was rare, when Dave or myself couldn't remember our lines, or when she couldn't look at us because we were morons, just laughing. And then John Stamos would comment, 'Candace and I are the only ones who know our stuff here.' If she messed up, she was very humble. She had a very self-effacing attitude about it all. Candace was just always a pro.

"Everyone loved the honesty Candace brought to her acting— how she seemed so real, not like someone playing a part. And often the parts reflected her very giving heart. Once on the show, she

The Full House *moms (from left):* Janice, Barb, Jarnie, Shari.

brought home a man with Alzheimer's—and that typified her heart off-screen as well. If she could love someone, she would. She had a sparkle and a light in her eyes that drew in those around her."

In the later years, she and Bob added Scott Weinger (Steve Hale) to make a trio of trouble. They'd go hang out together, especially to concerts.

Candace's schedule was very much like Kirk's. I moved between the sets to keep an eye on both kids and to always revel in the talent these kids had. The other two girls had talents I admired as well. Melissa had acting talent, but felt so self-conscious that she didn't want to use it. She also has the most beautiful singing voice. She could sing along with any of the popular vocalists, sounding very professional. She wanted to pursue voice in Nashville, which Robert and I encouraged, but again, she felt too shy—kind of like her mother, I guess. She did shine in the area of the heart, as did Bridgette. Their best gifts lay deep inside them, welling up as blessings for others. The compassion of Bridgette and the brightness of her spirit were like open arms to anyone near her, drawing them into a safe, caring place.

Critical to me was that the kids would not buy into the whole Hollywood mindset. To counteract the insidious threads of pride—encouraged by the pampering actors received—I worked hard to keep them rooted in reality. When they changed out of wardrobe at the end of a shoot, I would not allow them to throw their clothes on the couch or the floor. This surprised the wardrobe people. "Oh, you don't have to hang up your clothes; that's my job!" they would say.

I insisted that it was their job to provide the clothes to be worn, not to clean up my child's mess when he or she was through with the outfits.

I also insisted the kids clean their dressing rooms before we left for the day. They understood that the room was home for the week, and Mom was around to make sure they treated it that way. As far as I was concerned, their chores needed to be done just as if they were at home.

I taught and modeled how they were to treat the Craft food person with the same respect as they did the studio producer, with the same respect that they did the extras and the extras' parents. Robert did, as well, when he came on the set. He was known by all as being a very direct man with no hidden agendas. He, too, was very well liked by crew members. He loved to tease them and felt more comfortable with the crew than with anyone else. Together, they were all just guys horsing around.

Both Robert and I continually reminded our children that they needed to be giving generously out of their abundance—not only financially, but also out of their abundance of love and kindness showered on them everywhere they went. I would not allow my children to *ever* disrespect anyone, or to look down on anyone.

At home, Kirk and Candace were treated just like the other two children. They did their chores, took out the trash, kept their rooms clean, and picked up after themselves alongside Melissa and Bridgette. Sometimes we had to make adjustments in their chore schedule as their filming schedule filled up, knowing that they were carrying a full load. Honestly, with shoots, school, and chores at home, they were logging just as many hours as an adult could handle. Robert and I always made sure we were communicating with them and making sure they seemed okay.

Truth is, I kept a pretty close eye on them at all times, and I would have pulled them out with a snap of my fingers if I sensed they were struggling with anything. Nothing was worth the decay of my children's well-being.

Schooling for Kirk and Candace was a bit of a challenge for a while. When they were in commercials, they brought homework to the set. Once they started acting regularly with guest appearances on a show, or working with movies, we found that some of the public school teachers were very cooperative and some were not.

"Just give instructions on what you want my kid to know," Robert told the teachers, "and I'll make sure to get it to the studio teachers. I'll pick up the work and I'll drop it off. All I ask of you is for you to let me know what work that will be."

We couldn't understand why some uncooperative teachers were so reluctant to give us work. It made our efforts to keep the kids up with their classes very difficult. The ones who did cooperate made our lives so much easier.

To add to the problems, the more Candace appeared on television, the more cruel her classmates became. Unfortunately, Candace was often at the receiving end of painful episodes at school. One day seven girls came up behind her and each grabbed a chunk of her long, blond hair and yanked her to the ground. Another day, as Candace knelt before her locker, girls again yanked her hair so hard that she fell over backwards. One time, the kids ruined her locker so she couldn't open it. Jealous kids also squirted shaving cream through the vents of her locker to ruin the items inside. Chewed gum stretched out all over the outside like a gray spider web, attached to the handle and smeared over it.

When the pranks escalated and could not seem to be stopped, we took her out of public school and put her in a private school.

Robert didn't like doing that. He worked for the public school system and felt the system was good enough for his kids. But enough was enough. And we both agreed this was the best choice under the circumstances.

Even sadder was that we did not know that similar things were happening to Melissa. Kids threw her to the ground, kicked her in the head, kneed her in the back, and threatened to beat her up every day of every year in that high school. Someone wrote an obscene, profane note about Kirk on her desk. But she never said anything to anyone but her friends whom she begged to meet her before and after school to protect her. It would be years before she finally confessed to us in a sobbing outburst that the only thing she wished for was to go to a new school. Although we immediately enrolled her in a different school, by then she was a senior and had already endured so much cruelty.

Candace had asked to stay in public school once she reached middle school in order to be with her friends and have a social life. Her first two years on the set, she received studio schooling. Then we arranged for her to take a couple of classes in the morning at public school before coming to the set. However, she still had to put in her required time on the set, which meant that when the other kids were done with school, she still had work to do. She didn't always enjoy the fact that when everyone else got to play during breaks, she had to go back to the tiny little classroom to do her work. After ninth grade, she went back to studio school alone, where a teacher we had chosen taught her.

Barbara, Kirk, and Robert at Kirk's graduation from Chatsworth High School in 1988.

Once both shows really took hold, Robert and I were able to choose the studio teacher we wanted—a fabulous one named Glen Woodmansee. We had seen him work with other kids and liked what we saw. He was brilliant, quirky, fun for the kids. He knew the studio system well, and was very flexible in his teaching, able to get the kids working on their schoolwork in the sometimes-short bursts they had available. Glen did well with maintaining the balance between enforcing the health and welfare child laws, and being flexible with production.

Glen had Candace write her own newspaper, so she would learn research, observational skills, writing, editing, math (for layout), and art (for design)—and have fun doing it! Together they probably published five issues of the *Full Mouse Times*, which had a little picture of a mouse on the front page. Candace wrote articles, funny tidbits, puzzles, quizzes, and copied the style of some articles from teen magazines. Candace would pick a "bachelor of the month"—say, the prop master—and ask teeny-bopper questions and run the interview in the issue. After a couple of issues, they ran low on material. So they asked the other child actors in shows on the lot to use their classroom time to contribute articles. Soon kids from *Full House*, *Family Matters, Step by Step*, and *Hangin' with Mr. Cooper* had bylines in the *Full Mouse Times*, which was then distributed to all the family show sitcoms on the lot.

Glen even brought in a special trailer for the kids to do science projects. We loved the one-on-one attention the kids got for their schooling. Robert decided that if they lacked in one area, they were now earning the funds to later hire a subject-specific tutor who could get them up to speed to be prepared for college.

Kirk : I loved school. I liked the one-on-one time with the teacher, as well as the interaction with my studio siblings. He made it fun, and being with my friends also made it fun. Sometimes we'd be separated from each other for special age-appropriate classes, but otherwise, we got to study together as well as act together.

Candace : The hardest part about being in studio school is that you're stuck in box of a classroom with a teacher for a solid three hours.

Candace seemed to connect well with adults, probably because of the show and being around adults most of the time. She got their jokes like she got her father's. Bob Saget says, "I'm very quirky, but Candace understands those quirks and loves me anyway."

I loved hearing Jeff Franklin say that Candace was easy to work with, had a great spirit about her, and was always very professional. There was nothing forced about her acting. Nothing fake. "Candace was always the most prepared. I gave her fewer acting notes than anyone else in the cast. On her own, she always found the right spot and the right place to play, whatever the material—she didn't need to be told." Her strong work ethic and her bright spirit helped her to be well received by the other cast members.

She was also well received by the fans.

The creator of *Full House* says, "She's very funny. But she's also someone who kids completely related to. You always heard from everyone that they especially loved DJ. They felt she was real, a real girl. She came off as someone they all would want to be friends with and hang out with."

And it was true! Later in the show's life, Candace was traveling around, doing appearances all over the country and Canada. She had cut her hair pretty short. At the next appearance only a few days after the show aired, thousands of girls came to meet DJ Tanner—all sporting short hairdos. "I cut my hair because you did," so many told her.

The *Full House* set was like having lots of little kids on the show. Even Bob Saget admits John, Dave, and he were like a bunch of eleven-year-old boys when they got on the set.

The environment was always lighthearted and playful. Everyone on the show loved to laugh, and loved to make each other laugh. So these grown-up boys made jokes like most little ones. They really liked to get the girls to dissolve in giggles. Sometimes, though, the jokes got more than a little off-color, and we mothers and the studio teacher banded together to talk with the show runner, who would then remind the "boys" that there were young girls on the set. They'd be very good—for a few days.

It seemed that funny situations and laughter followed this show. Bob Saget said, "We often had animals on the show. And animals on the set behaved as, well, animals on the set," and the crew found those

Andrea Barber, Jodie Sweetin, Candace, and Mary-Kate and Ashley Olsen at the Hollywood Christmas Parade.

things hilarious. "Missed lines, unusual guests making appearances, funny faces—anything brought a laugh."

"Sometimes the general foibles we all have would cause great laughter," Bob says. "Jodie's phase where she kept tripping, for example." Or the reactions of the actors in real-life situations. During an earthquake, Bob led Jodie and Candace to safety underneath the big, heavy outer door. However, Dave sought safety under the arch leading to the girls' room on the set. "Right, Dave," Bob said. "When the lights come crashing down on the *paper* arch, it's going to split it in two, with you along with it." The cast and crew got laughs out of that for days.

Yet it wasn't all silly. There were serious issues dealt with as well. On *Full House*, the writers and show creator also asked Candace and me to share with them the things Candace encountered in real life. They wanted the show to be very accurate in how a teen girl feels. We dealt with many issues on the show. If we felt something wasn't accurate or if Candace was uncomfortable, then the writers would make appropriate adjustments. That pleased me.

Bob fondly remembers that "Candace always got the scenes that required an honest conversation, and me playing the straighter, morality-based dad, she and I would have some of the more poignant one-on-one conversations on that show. She always had the voice of reason in her character on and off camera."

Candace, now a regular in a series, began having quite a bit of money that was not going into a trust. Robert did not want the kids spending it at their age or losing it. So he found ways to invest, and decided to invest some of Candace's money in real estate.

"Candace," he said to her one evening. "I was thinking about investing some of your earnings in a cabin for the family at Big Bear. Would you like that?"

She nodded eagerly. We'd been to Big Bear, a mountain resort community only two hours from our home, for Candace to act in a Disney film. We'd liked it so much, we rented a cabin for Thanksgiving one year, then for the Christmas holiday, and we'd all enjoyed it.

So Robert took trips up to Big Bear to look at cabins there. He'd have me come up when he'd isolated a few. I felt like Baby Bear— some were too big, and some were too small. One day, we walked into the real estate office and saw one that had just come on the market. We drove to see it and held our breath. It looked good. When we stepped inside, I immediately knew it was just right. The owner wanted to sell the house with everything in it so he could travel unencumbered. We couldn't have been more delighted. Baby Bear found her new retreat home.

On June 22, 1969, Barbara became Mrs. Robert Cameron. Here she is with her new mother-in-law, Helen. (Note the Spanish mantilla.)

Barbara's sister Lynda was the Maid of Honor. Friend Louise Pierce and Barb's sister Joanne were bride's maids.

Kirk doing a hand-balancing act with his Uncle David, Robert's brother.

Sweethearts Barbara and Robert.

Bridgette, Robert, and Barbara.

Kirk and Andrew Rock picketing Robert for some perceived mistreatment...

Steve Garvey and Kirk at a Dodgers game (1979 or 1980).

*Bridgette, Adam Rich, Melissa, and Candace (front) at the
Youth in Films Awards, 1984.*

From top: *Meegan, Andrew, Ryan, Bridgette, Jennifer, and Melissa.*

Ryan Rock and Candace enjoy Sunday at the beach.

Jodie Sweetin and Candace in Las Vegas filming an episode of Full House.

Andrea Barber, Jodie Sweetin, and Candace poolside at one of our family parties.

Barb's family (from left): Carol, Lynda, Frank, Barb, Joanne, and their parents, Jeanne and Frank Bausmith.

chapter 13

Bonbons and Business

My kids settled into a routine they thoroughly enjoyed, and so did I. Sitting in the bleachers, watching my kids rehearse, interact with those around them, or act on either set filled my heart with bursting joy. I continually thanked God for these things that I did not deserve. I didn't know why God was being so good to me.

But all was not perfect. Although I didn't find the love I was looking for at the studios, I found a decent replacement. I felt so good while on the sets. It didn't matter that I didn't feel loved at home.

Problems at home spread beyond Robert. I didn't always get along with my girls—we didn't seem to "get" each other, and so I continually felt awkward in our attempts to connect. If they came to me with a problem that concerned boys, I became fearful and wanted to be sure they knew the seriousness of going too far. Once, when Jeremy Miller (Ben on *Growing Pains*) called to tell Candace he liked her, I scolded her for being too young to have a boyfriend, instead of letting this little crush play out in innocence. I tried to give Bridgette and Melissa a lecture on "the birds and the bees." They rolled their eyes, and Melissa said, "Mo-o-om, we already know about that."

On the set, I was known as a good, normal mom—not a stage mom. The difference between the two is well known in the industry. A stage mom insists everyone treats her little darling like the king and tyrant and the superstar of the show—even if he isn't. Whatever her precious wants, he gets. No one is to speak to this child with anything but humble respect. Some of these moms also behave as though they, rather than their children, are the stars.

People who work with child actors have a constant fear of losing their jobs if the parent or even the child complains. The crew would go out of their way to please, so much so that I sometimes wanted to gag!

On the other hand, a normal mom is one who realizes that this actor is still a child and still needs the guidance of an adult. A normal mom tries to facilitate what needs to be done to help the process of getting a show done, rather than get in the way. This kind of mom listens to the director and producer to hear what is expected of her child, and helps the child fulfill those expectations.

However, being a mom also means that you watch your child for signs of illness, fatigue, and exhaustion, and keep them protected. After all, although the series producers we had were always concerned for the children, they might get caught up in their jobs and not see the signs Mom would see.

I really and truly cared for these people who surrounded my children every day. They all worked so hard and became like family to us. And so, I treated them as you would any family member. I either made or arranged for cakes to be delivered for every occasion possible. I wanted to celebrate the birthdays on the set, and also to recognize those who had done a good job—whether they had been a gaffer or grip, long-term guest actor or writer.

When doing a show that lasts seven to eight years, a lot of life takes place. People come and go and have wonderful things to celebrate. There are also the hard times when someone gets sick or a loved one passes away. I didn't want those things to go unacknowledged either. I found meaningful cards, and took them around to get notes and signatures from others for the person enduring tough times.

People wanted and needed to be seen, recognized, and valued, and I wanted to be sure that everyone knew that others cared. And I could easily orchestrate that. I could be the arms big enough to hug everyone and draw them in so they didn't feel left out. It wasn't difficult. I didn't do it for show. I did it because I knew the pain of being invisible, and because I really did care about each person I met.

In turn, Hollywood filled me up like nothing I'd ever experienced. All the gaps and holes inside me, left by Robert, closed when I walked into the studio on tape nights, baskets of chocolate cookies hanging off my arms and dangling from my hands. It pleased me no end to hear reverberate through the set, "The cookie lady's here!" and see those forty-eight dozen cookies snatched up by the eager cast and crew and hoarded in a favorite hiding place.

I absorbed all the attention I received from cast, crew, other moms, and even the audience.

If I'd really been self-aware, I might have seen that this attention on the sets numbed the parts of me that were so hungry for something more. I'd given up on Robert ever loving me the way I wanted to be loved. But inside I still desperately craved that elusive love. Going to the set relieved the pain for a while, filling me up with something else—importance.

At home, the lack of my husband's love, the strain of not connecting with my children, and my own perceived deficiencies as a person filled the house. At home I didn't feel valued. These driving forces remained hidden, but powerful. At least on the set, I received all that I missed. And I was somebody special. At home I was a mom, I was a wife, but my marriage wasn't the way I dreamed it should be, so I escaped to the studio and got to see how others lived, having conversations with people about other kinds of things.

Robert didn't value the work I did with the kids, either. "You're just sitting around eating bonbons. You might as well be at home watching soap operas for all the productivity you have."

Yet the ways I was productive were entirely different than what he would notice. I learned so much about the business and the people in it. I learned how to play the games, how to be myself in a society-within-a-society that encouraged sameness. I learned how to be close and break down barriers erected to keep out everyone and everything in this world of backstabbing. I learned about the world of entertainment, about this life in a very different hemisphere than where I lived. I learned what worked and what didn't in negotiating, talking, acting, and stage presence. I unknowingly learned lessons that would be critical to my future.

Sure, some days I sat for six hours in the hot bleachers, by myself, just watching. Other days were filled with the chatter of moms. But my job as manager meant I also had to ensure my kids got what they needed. I dealt with the producers of the show, negotiating, talking, and standing up for my kids. Neither the producers nor I liked this part very much. But we all respected one another for the jobs we were required to do. Managers, no matter who they are, are considered roadblocks to the show getting done. The producer needed to be sure that all the requirements of the studio and the production company were met. I had to be sure that all the needs of my children were being met. Hence, my very existence was a roadblock. Anytime I approached the producers, an invisible wall immediately rose between us.

If my kids felt uncomfortable with the script, off I went to the producer, who would then defend the writer. The attitude of the writers was, "Just say the line. You're only an actor. You're not really that person." But my kids, especially Kirk, wanted to be good role models for the viewers, and felt that some things should not be said. So we had many battles to fight. But when the work was done, I left that part of my life behind, and became Barbara, the person again.

This shift isn't normal in Hollywood. What's normal is to keep to yourself and protect your own interests. With thousands of people after only a handful of jobs, it's critical to be all business, all the time.

It's also often not how well you work, or how hard you work, but whether or not you're on the winning or losing team at the moment. So many people want into this business, but they don't realize how cutthroat it is. Few friends are made, because everyone is a potential enemy, or a competitor. It's a very empty, bloodthirsty business.

I refused to live that way. And so I made a constant effort to be kind, to care about the people, and to try to get them connecting on a level deeper than what was going on onstage. Many I never got through to, but others slowly lowered the Hollywood defense mechanism and let me inside. One person in particular has become a lifelong friend. While on the set, he was all stern and unsmiling. Robert would go up to him and tease him about it, but he wouldn't break. Yet off-set, or on the weekends, we'd hang out and have a great time.

It took me a while to learn all these things about the industry. It ran counterculture to everything I had been taught, believed, understood, and lived for. And I was not about to let the industry change me — or my children. Certainly I didn't make it a conscious point to change the system. All I knew is that I needed to manage my kids' careers very well to protect them from the Hollywood monster that destroyed so many child actors who made it big. I needed to manage those careers daily—to be on top of everything that was happening to them and around them. I needed to pay attention to things that seemed very small, because in this business, small things can have far-reaching ramifications. Much of what I did, was done only out of fierce mother-bear instinct.

As manager, I also read scripts, ran lines, set up appointments, and made travel plans. As Kirk became more popular, the demands on his time became greater, and my job grew more intensive. Our relationship started to become strained because I was always around— and what teenager wants his mom there every time he turns around? I traveled with him and discussed business with him, and it became more of a business relationship than that of a mother and son. Changing my outfits when I changed my rolls was helpful. We had a great relationship, just not a typical one.

When *Full House* began to really take on a large, loyal audience as well, I flew all over the country and Canada for publicity with Candace and our assistant, Jonathan Koch, whom we lovingly called Jono. On these trips, I made sure she was safe, well fed, taken care of, and got her sleep.

While I managed the kids, Robert's tension with the girls at home grew to a breaking point. "Bridgette is so dumb," he said for the hundredth time one night, as we got ready for bed. "She'll be lucky to graduate from high school. I don't think she'll ever get her diploma."

"She is not dumb," I said. "Maybe she has a learning disability. Maybe we should have her tested."

Robert sat on the edge of the bed and ran his fingers through his hair. He sighed. "Okay. I'll arrange it."

The expert who tested Bridgette said what we should have seen all along in her. "Bridgette will never be a good student," he told us, as we sat across the desk from him, not touching or looking at each other. "She does, however, have a very tender heart. She's one of the happiest children I've tested. I wouldn't worry about her anymore. Just get her through school. She's probably not college-bound, but that's okay. She's going to do just fine in life."

I glanced over at Robert. His shoulders drooped forward, his gaze toward his shoes. I knew he'd feel sad. College was his most important

Melissa, Bridgette, and Candace enjoy working with Kirk on the Halloween episode of Growing Pains.

dream for his children. Knowing one child would not be going probably made him fear for her future.

In the car on the way home, Robert held the wheel, tapping his thumbs against it. He stared at a red light, waiting for it to change. "I can't deal with homework supervision anymore, Barb."

An idea flashed through me. I felt so silly. Why hadn't I thought of it before? The answer seemed so simple. "Why don't we get the girls a tutor?"

He looked at me, then back at the light, shifting into first gear as it changed. After a couple blocks of silence, he said, "Okay. We can try it."

That decision fixed so much.

First, Robert took Bridgette aside and said, "Honey, I know school is hard for you. But let's just work on getting your diploma, okay?"

Second, we found the most amazing tutor, Sara Getzkin, through Kelly Gursey, an acquaintance of Candace, Bridgette and Melissa. They had met Kelly at the gym. Kelly and Sara, being great friends since middle school, hung out, shopped, and generally did girl stuff together. Kelly introduced the girls to Sara one summer day after having talked to her about them. Even though Sara and Kelly were college age, they enjoyed being with these young teen and pre-teen girls. My girls had so much energy and excitement about them. They loved to shop, and needed someone to cart them around. Besides, Kelly and Sara loved helping them with makeup, clothes, and girl talk. They were like big sisters to my girls. They were a huge help that summer, helping the girls shop everywhere for the right outfits, jewelry, shoes, bags—everything a girl needs—for Bridgette's Sweet Sixteen birthday celebration in the early fall.

Not long before the party, Robert and I took Sara to a Chinese restaurant, where Robert did his usual fabulous job of asking questions. He loved his daughters dearly and wanted to be protective of them. He wanted to be sure this new person in their lives was there for a good reason. "What school do you go to? Where do you work? What are you planning to do after Community College? Why do you like hanging around my girls?"

He liked her answers—her dedication to school and working hard, not to mention her upbeat spirit and connection with the girls. He offered her a job tutoring the girls four days a week, two hours a day. Sara went home to consider and talk it over with her parents. When she accepted, we were delighted.

Sara brought to the girls a sweet spirit. I'm sure it was tough for her to juggle her friendship with them and the newly appointed authority. But the girls loved her and listened to her. Sara went through the school assignments every day, looking for ways to be creative. She rewarded Bridgette's reading a book by showing her a movie about the book or a related subject. She helped her do a Social Studies project on apartheid. Kirk joined in, filming the project. Together they turned it into a smashing success. She made games out of things to help Bridgette stay on task and get the information she needed. Afterwards, the girls would go off to the gym or shopping. Sara stayed for dinner often, becoming a solid member of the family.

The girls and Robert were much happier with the situation, and I preferred coming home to a calm household each night.

As much as it seemed I was a woman on my own, I still didn't believe in myself, or trust myself. I still looked to Robert to tell me what was right and wrong, what to do in the situations outside my managing world. Robert seemed so frustrated with me much of the time because I was continually down on myself and didn't communicate well with him or the kids. He wanted to help, but didn't know how. He'd heard from someone how much the very popular and well-attended Erhard Seminars Training (est) had helped people. He encouraged me, bolstered by his friend, that est would be a place where I would find a solution to many of my issues through self-awareness. Desperate to do something that would improve our relationship for the better, I agreed to go when Robert suggested it. I trusted Robert as my older husband, and thought all the arguments for going sounded like good reasons. And I did want to do whatever I could to change our marriage. I knew that the mess we were in wasn't all Robert's fault. I hoped that at est, I might find clues in how to communicate better with Robert, and how to fix myself so he would be happier.

The day I went, I drove with my heart in my throat, clutching the steering wheel. Apprehension filled me. I wished I didn't have to go alone. But, as always, I figured others knew best for me, and I would be the good, obedient girl, in spite of my fears.

Inside the large room, the facilitator gave instructions. I sat, stunned at the rigidity of the rules. I felt trapped and afraid. There was something about what others might call the "aura" of the room. And I didn't like it. Once the process started, I found some of it kind of interesting, and some of it kind of weird. As much as I wanted to really find help there, as the morning progressed, the realization grew that something wasn't right. Fear grew inexplicably inside, and I had to get out. But they had people guarding the doors so no one could leave.

At the first break, I found my van and high-tailed it for home. The whole way, I kept looking in my rearview mirror, afraid that one of their people would follow me and make me go back. When I got home, Robert, his sister Margaret, and her friend were sitting at the table, having a grand old time. When I walked in, I bet it looked like I'd seen a ghost.

"What are you doing here?" Robert asked.

I broke down and cried.

Margaret said, "What's wrong?"

"She was supposed to be at est," Robert told them.

"I went there," the friend said. "I loved it."

I felt stupid, but I couldn't shake the sense that something was terribly wrong there. But I couldn't tell them that. "I felt trapped," I wanted to say. Instead, I said, "It's just not for me."

"I'm sorry it was bad for you," Margaret said, making room for me on the kitchen bench. "Maybe you can try again."

Not a chance. I forced a smile, hoping that would keep everyone from knowing I had no intention of going back.

If things were going to change within me and within my marriage, it must happen an entirely different way. I desperately wanted that change, but didn't know where to look, or how to begin making that change happen.

chapter 14

The Hollywood Dream

When body surfing, at the crest of a wave, there is a moment when it almost seems as though there's a pause, right before the adrenaline-rushing momentum catapults you toward the beach.

Once Candace settled into *Full House*, our family began the exciting ride of Hollywood. I never dreamed what lay ahead of us. And if I had, I would have been more excited than a kid going to Disneyland for the first time. Life was fun and full of the most excitement anyone could ever imagine. One big perk after another. The whirlwind snatches you up, and you're off for a glorious spin. Unlike Dorothy's ride in the tornado, this ride couldn't have been more fun. The Camerons? At the top of the Hollywood game? Never in a million years.

And yet, here we were. Appearances, TV specials, trips to location, recognition, fan events, money for the kids, hobnobbing with great stars, and yes, even Kirk meeting the president. The kids especially loved the red-carpet events, smiling as the paparazzi cameras flashed and reporters called out their names. Although I rarely let them go to parties, there were some associated with the shows where all the current celebrities attended. Dressing up, being picked up from the house in a limo—high stuff for a kid ... and not too bad for Mom, either.

Opposite page: *Robin Williams, Kirk, Kurt Russell, and Barbara during the filming of* The Best of Times.

Often at these events, the stars are happy and friendly. Although the conversations don't go deep, they can be full of laughter and gaiety. So for the evening, spirits are high—a kind of happy drug infusing the parties.

The kids got to choose their favorite clothes from the season's wardrobe to take home. They received fun gifts from the cast and crew of the shows, and every Christmas Iris gave them each something special.

And as manager, wherever my kids went, I usually went. And most of the time, whoever my kids met, I met.

The roster of who we met could fill chapters. The biggest names on television, in movies, in politics in the '80s and '90s—all these were people we ran across in the greater part of our show lives. Robin Williams, Dudley Moore, Janet Jackson, Eddie Murphy, Julie Andrews, James Garner, Brooke Shields, Tony Danza, Patty Duke, Michael Douglas, Jamie Gertz, Terri Garr, Don Johnson, Mariette Hartley, Betty White, Eric Stoltz, Mary Stuart Masterson, Tony Orlando, Telly Savalas, and Leonardo DiCaprio—to name only a very few.

One or both of my kids appeared on talk shows with hosts like Oprah, Johnny Carson, Phil Donahue, Sally Jesse Rafael, Vickie Lawrence, Joan Rivers, Regis and Kathy Lee, and on other morning shows across America. Some of these shows included me, and Bridgette and Melissa were sometimes either on stage or in the audience.

Bridgette got to do work in front of the camera as she'd always longed to do—as an extra—sometimes with lines and sometimes without. She had bit parts and appearances on *Growing Pains*, *Full House*, and *Home Improvement*.

It seemed that as Kirk's fame grew, he took the lot of us along. Magazines and television specials began to discuss the whole Cameron family.

Melissa : Kids would come up to me in school or out on the road and say, "You're Melissa Cameron, your middle name is Rachelle, your birthday is October 3rd and your favorite color is blue." It was like they knew more about me than I did!

We haven't seen that phenomenon in any other sibling actors. You might know about the siblings who are both actors, but you don't hear much about the entire family—the non-acting siblings and the parents—being interviewed equally, nor treated as a whole family unit. Sure, many are mentioned, but usually as one pitted against the other.

One Mother's Day special even filmed our family in the backyard of our home.

Bridgette : It was too weird. Dad's barbecuing in the background while the rest of us sit around a table and are supposed to be acting naturally. Yeah, like we have film crews in our backyard all the time.

It seemed everyone wanted to know what the Cameron family was up to. If anyone tried to interview me about my *two* children, I always informed them that I was the proud mother of *four* children—including Bridgette and Melissa.

Robert frequently felt intimidated by people with money. As a schoolteacher on a small salary, he was afraid people were looking down on him. So, in the beginning, he often stayed in the background. After a while, he noticed that a lot of these stars felt awkward as well—many of them insecure and self-conscious with people looking at them

Barbara and Candace (center) on a talk show.

Barb with Telly Savalas.

all the time. That broke the ice for him, and he began to be himself — dry humor and all. If they didn't like him, too bad.

Both Robert and I couldn't believe some of the people who would sit at our table at some event or another, and who surrounded us. Betty White, "I don't get no respect" Rodney Dangerfield, George Burns, Danny Thomas. The list goes on and on. And what really made Robert crazy was the fact that Kirk often had no clue about the actors he rubbed shoulders with.

For example, Kirk did a Bob Hope special with Lucille Ball, Phyllis Diller, Don Johnson, Brooke Shields, and the president of the United States, Ronald Reagan. Kirk got his picture taken shaking hands with the president, but remembers nothing about it!

On that show, Kirk did a skit with Lucille Ball where he hid inside a trunk for a magic trick. Lucille pulled all sorts of silly things from the trunk, making her goofy faces all the while, until she then pulled out Kirk.

Not too much later, Lucille Ball died. When the "greats" of comedy put on a tribute for her, they asked Kirk to come and be part of the show. Afterwards, Kirk rode in the car with Danny Thomas to Bob Hope's house where he would have dinner with Danny, Bob, George Burns, Phyllis Diller, Jimmy Stewart, and others. Robert and I could have clobbered Kirk. He had no idea whose company he was in. To him, they were just a bunch of old people telling dumb stories about a cat they couldn't get out from under the house. They thought the story was hysterical.

Kirk, instead of being honored (at the time) says, "I'm sitting there watching dentures falling out of their mouths, thinking, "What's with the old guys?" I remember riding in the car with Danny Thomas because he had a pistol in his glove compartment."

Kirk was asked to endorse many products, and received a lot of free stuff for many reasons—people wanting him to endorse their product, people liking him, people wanting to impress him. Many times if Kirk showed up unexpectedly at a food establishment, the manager gave him a free meal, and sometimes meals for his guests as well. One man wanted Kirk to appear at an event for him, didn't have cash to pay him, and offered him a car instead.

Car show events frequently asked stars to come as a draw to get people to lay down their hard-earned cash and come see vintage autos, or classic autos, or new autos, or a combination thereof. They paid these actors to come sign photos, sometimes next to the real draw for the men—Playboy bunnies.

Darling Kirk and his great smile caught the attention of Playboy Bunny Julie McCullough. They chatted and laughed at the events where they appeared together.

After one, Julie called Kirk and invited him to come out to the Playboy Mansion for a party.

"Hey, man, go for it!" Robert said, high-fiving Kirk. "You won't get this chance again."

"Don't you dare," I growled, hoping Kirk would see both mother-bear, as well as stern manager. "If something were to happen while you were there—no matter how innocent—and someone took a picture of you, they could construe all sorts of lies. An event like this could haunt you for years to come." I took a breath and looked right at him. "Besides, I don't want you to go."

Kirk looked from his thumbs-up father to his glowering mother. "If you're not home by dinner," I said, "then I'll know you went." Kirk came home at six.

Kirk: I was sixteen, and scared about what would happen there. Deep down, I knew that if my mom thought it was a bad idea, it probably was. And I didn't want to upset her. I probably made it off like it was an excuse. If you don't want me to go, then I won't go. But deep down inside, I wanted an excuse to get out of it. As much as I didn't let it show, I respected her very much.

I laugh now, wondering if Robert is secretly disappointed to this day.

Kirk had a lot of fun on his own, too. One of the cameramen worked on *Growing Pains* as well as on *Family Ties,* starring Michael J. Fox. Turns out that Michael was a prankster as well, and had heard about Kirk through the cameraman. One day Michael showed up at Kirk's school trailer. "Hey, Kirk," he said, "can you break away for a few minutes?"

Kirk checked with his teacher, and took off.

They both hopped into Michael's black Ferrari and started tooling down the streets of Burbank. They loved stopping at the signals and waiting for the carloads of girls next to them to notice the two grinning stars in the hot car next to them. They'd grin, wave, take off, and do it again at another light.

Having people notice you, like you, desire to be with you, hang on every word you say is almost like a drug. It's easy to get addicted. And it's also weird being a kid, knowing you're a kid, and having all these adults drooling over your every move. The result is a kind of odd growing up. In some ways my acting kids were far more mature than kids their own age, and in other ways, they were more immature with their cloistered, staged life as a star.

Sometimes Kirk thrived on all the attention, and sometimes he hated it. As a teenager, it's horrible to have people expect you to be perfect all the time, and to be this unreal person who doesn't truly exist. When a teenager gets pimples, it's bad enough to endure a day at regular school. But as a star, every pimple is noticed by the entire country! Everything you wear is not just scrutinized by your school peers, but by a vicious group of reporters and paparazzi just waiting to catch you on an off day. Being a teenager is hard enough, but being a teenager with an entire country, and sometimes *world* watching can be terribly unnerving and disconcerting.

Candace didn't mind being in the limelight or growing up on a show. To her, the show was a second family and a second home. She'd been acting since she was five, so she knew this world best. However, she did feel self-conscious about going through puberty on camera, in front of a nation. And she really hated that everything seemed to focus on her weight. The first thing out of people's mouths seemed to be something about her weight. People made rude comments to her (and still do) about how fat she was on the show, or that she was so chubby. She, like many teen girls, had fluctuating weight during that part of her growing-up years. Other than that, being a very outgoing, friendly girl, she thoroughly enjoyed meeting fans and talking with them, signing autographs.

Bridgette and Melissa had childhoods that were normal in one aspect—they went to public school, came home, did their homework—but in another, they didn't. They had superstar siblings who got lots of money and lots of attention. And because of their siblings, they got to travel to places and do things they never could have done on their father's simple salary.

At school, Melissa and Bridgette found it a bit odd to see their brother's poster in other kids' lockers, pictures on their notebooks, and some even wearing T-shirts with his photo on it. They often didn't know who their real friends were.

Melissa : Sometimes kids would be really nice and then say, "Can I come over and meet your brother?"

You develop radar as to who was really a friend and who wasn't. Most of my friends I'd had since way before Kirk became popular. The kids I liked the best were the ones who would be honest that they liked the show, thought Kirk was cute, but would still like to get to know me and be my friend.

I think we all loved the traveling that came with celebrity status. We probably visited every major city in every state in the nation, with many smaller ones in between. We were treated like royalty wherever we went. I was very proud of my children and their manners—just like when they were little, they remembered their "please" and "thank you," looking people in the eye, and engaging them whenever possible.

The kids were in virtually every Hollywood Christmas parade for all the years they were on shows. Candace was in the Tournament of Roses Parade and the Macy's Thanksgiving Day Parade.

On the rare occasion when I couldn't travel with Kirk, Robert or a family friend would accompany him to various parts of the world.

Kirk played tennis in a pro-am tournament with the Prince of Monaco, Arancha Sanchez, and Michael Chang, staying in palatial digs while there. All expenses paid, of course.

Candace, Robert, and I flew to Ecuador for a pro-am tennis tournament with Pancho Gonzalez, after which we visited the Galapagos Islands—none of which we would have ever been able to do on our own.

The cast of *Full House* joined the Beach Boys concert in front of thousands at the Los Angeles Coliseum, singing and dancing and having a great time.

Robert and Kirk flew to Acapulco, Mexico, in a private Lear jet so Kirk could perform a little song-and-dance routine with Bob Hope called "One Hot Tamale."

Someone came up with the "great" idea for a skit, where a line of beautiful girls would each come and give Kirk a kiss. What no one told Kirk was that the girls had decided to up the ante. Pretty soon, to Kirk's surprise and embarrassment, many girls surrounded him, all planting kisses on him at once.

And then, Robert and Kirk decided to "surprise Mom" with a filmed skit of their own. Robert sat on a low beach chair in the surf, while the same bevy of beautiful bikini-clad girls swarmed Robert, pressing their bodies against him, cooing and fluttering all over him while he laughed and Kirk filmed. Let's just say that I was not amused. For me, it was yet another slap in the face.

On location with Full House *in Hawaii (1989): Melissa, Sara Getzkin, Candace, Robert, Barb, Jodie Sweetin, Bridgette, and Janice Sweetin (Jodie's mom).*

Kirk won the People's Choice award two years in a row for Favorite Young Television Performer. His face appeared on the cover of at least one teen magazine every month for four years running—either a small photo or the full cover shot. His popularity exploded, turning our quiet family life upside down and inside out.

Kirk's rise to fame benefited all of us. Need a seat in a restaurant? Have Kirk call and the best seat in the house instantly became available.

If he had to go on location, it was required by law for him to have a parent or guardian with him. When I could, I negotiated our two first-class tickets into five or six coach-class. Then all of us would get to go. When we flew anywhere with him, the flight attendants fell over themselves to make sure we were well attended to. Although this was excellent service, I felt really sad for the people around us who didn't have the same service just because they weren't on television.

On location, Kirk had to work, while the rest of us could shop, play, or enjoy the scenery.

Hawaii was the family favorite—compliments of both *Growing Pains* and *Full House*. Each child got to take a friend. Candace wanted to take Sara, the tutor. We all loved having her anywhere we went, and she doubled as a chaperone for the girls.

It seemed that every time I went to the grocery store, I'd see one of my kids, if not both, on a magazine cover. Of course, I felt proud. What mother wouldn't?

By now, Robert was finally realizing this fantasy thing was more than a fantasy—it was real. And on occasion he nudged a person in the grocery store line. "See that kid? Kirk Cameron? Yeah, he's sort of related. He's my son."

But at work, if his coworkers asked, "Are you related to Kirk Cameron?" He'd say, "No, no relation. Don't know the kid."

Eventually, someone found out and cornered him. "You're Kirk's dad, aren't you?"

By then, he wouldn't deny it. And suddenly his coworkers treated him differently. They would sidle up to him at odd times and begin to pour their hearts out to him, as though they were instant best buddies. This was a bit disconcerting at first, but then Robert took it on as something he could do to give to others who maybe didn't have anyone else to talk to.

Instead of spending money on boats, planes, and mansions—as most people thought we must be doing—we used savings from my salary to expand the tract home we'd been living in for years (and still live in today). Candace had been sleeping on a pullout sofa without complaint in the living room for years. It was time to get her a bedroom. Even after the small addition, Candace and Melissa shared a room.

We also used any savings to take Melissa and Bridgette with us on location, and take care of any needs they had.

We encouraged Candace and Kirk to spend their money wisely and modestly. They had their own money and used some of that to be generous to their siblings. Bridgette and Melissa were very excited when Candace would give them $100 for The Gap for Christmas, or on some other non-special occasion. Candace was very thoughtful, buying CDs for her sisters, or nice clothing from stores they could not have afforded.

Sometimes we would let them splurge. On Candace's first trip to New York, I gave her a spending limit and let her have a shopping spree in Macy's. In a photo of that day, she is beaming with Macy's bags hanging from her arms and sitting on the ground. She had bought a hat, shoes, and many other fun things a teen girl would love to have. We kept these occasions to a minimum, wanting the specialness of it to never go away.

Robert and I maintained our strict rules, however. We still insisted that all kids had a curfew. The acting kids had the same curfew as the others—and it was far earlier than most kids their age. And we didn't allow them to go to many Hollywood parties. We knew what went on at those parties, no matter how well chaperoned they were. The point of many of them was strictly in order to "be seen."

We did, however, give in and let Sara accompany the girls to a *Bop* party. The teen magazines often put on parties just so the paparazzi would have a chance to photograph the child stars and have something to put in their magazines. The girls were *so* excited to be able to go. And when they got there, they discovered the hot group, New Kids on the Block, was there. Being fans of the group, they couldn't wait to meet them. Funny thing was, everyone wanted to meet Candace! Since I didn't allow Candace or Kirk to go to the parties as a rule, no one really knew her, and wanted the chance to get close to her. The New Kids on the Block were fans of *Full House* and were just as excited to meet her. The group of them spent the entire evening talking and hitting it off. The New Kids loved my girls, telling them they were the most real people they had met. They got along so well, the girls invited them over for a barbecue at our house.

The whole family "went Hollywood" for Kirk's sixteenth birthday.

As much as I didn't want to buy into the Hollywood scene, I realize now how it crept into our lives without our knowing it. One example is the sixteenth birthday party we threw for Kirk and "five hundred of his closest friends." We rented out the largest ballroom at the Marriott Hotel, and decorated it with black, white, and silver balloons, and silver buckets filled with black and white popcorn. We hired the best DJ and came all decked out in black and silver lamé clothing. We had a blast, but I cringe now at the outrageous cost for the party. We simply thought that if your kid is on a hit television series, this is what you *do*.

We threw similar parties for the girls when they reached their "Sweet Sixteenth" and when Candace turned thirteen. The parties were smaller, but no less "done up" than Kirk's.

On the other hand, our kids had interests like other kids their age. For pets, Kirk owned snakes: a Burmese python named Dudley after Dudley Moore, and a red-tailed boa constrictor named Glen (a gift from the *Growing Pains* crew), as well as a tarantula named

Terminator. Out of his generosity, he gave the tarantula to the son of a friend who showed a fascination with the hairy spider. His single mother was mortified, but how could she say no to Kirk and the delight of her son?

Candace still had the sweet, tender heart of any typical girl, loving inanimate objects with an intensity most males will never understand. *TV's Bloopers and Practical Jokes* brought that out in an unexpected, very strong way.

The show came to us and wanted to play a joke on Candace when she was about thirteen years old. They set up a celebrity auction, asking for something of Kirk's and Candace's to auction off. They told Candace that they had called Robert, and he gave them items of theirs to auction off, but didn't say what the items were.

Kirk was in on the joke, and wore a hidden mike during the filming of the "auction." In the audience, Kirk leaned over to Candace and said, "I wonder what Dad gave them of ours to auction off."

Candace shrugged. She hadn't thought much about it. "Probably something from *Growing Pains* and *Full House*, like a picture or script or something," she whispered back.

The auctioneer came to Kirk's item, pulling out his treasured *Growing Pains* jacket! Kirk was in on the joke for Candace, but had no idea his father would give them the jacket as part of the joke. His shocked reaction was real. "No way!" he said, leaning over to Candace. "What was he thinking?"

Candace looked a little nervous. She said to him, "I wonder what Dad gave them of mine?"

She looked up, and the auctioneer held up her favorite little stuffed dog "Noopy." This dog was her security blanket. She didn't let anyone mistreat the dog, or even touch it. She stared, horrified that her most prized possession was about to be auctioned off and gone forever. "No, not Noopy!"

"It's okay, Candace. I'll get it. Whatever it costs, I'll buy it back."

Candace calmed down a little, her hopes up.

The bidding started and someone in the audience continually bid higher than Kirk. Finally, Kirk leaned over to Candace. "I'm so sorry, Can. I can't pay more than $500 for your dog. I just can't."

The bidding stopped, and a huge biker dude with chains, leathers, and arms like tree trunks sauntered toward the front. "Great, man!"

Kirk stopped him. "Look. There's been a mistake. My sister has cherished that since she was a little girl. You've gotta give it back."

"Naw," the guy said, "I really like that thing. It'll be a great ornament for my bike, man."

Candace stood by Kirk, sobbing hysterically. "Look, dude," Kirk said, "can I buy it back?"

"I really like it," the guy said. "I bought it fair and square."

"You see," Kirk pleaded, "my dad didn't know what he was doing. He made a mistake. Candace didn't give my dad permission to take it."

Candace shook, wracked with sobs.

Backstage, the producers gave the order in the buyer's hidden headset to give the dog back to her. Her reaction was so strong, they knew they would have to reshoot the piece if they couldn't get her under control. And they *never* reshot the jokes.

Finally, the guy said, "Okay, Candace can have it back. I'd hate to take something that she really loved."

The announcer said over the loudspeaker, "Next item to auction, dinner with the Cameron family." The rest of us—Robert, Bridgette, Melissa, and I—appeared from behind the stage curtain. "You're on *TV's Bloopers and Practical Jokes!*"

Candace obviously felt relieved that she had her precious dog back, and that it was only a joke. But her hysterical sobs were too much for the show and it looked like a cruel joke rather than the funny one they intended. So they reshot the whole thing after her initial reaction at seeing her dog. No one expected Candace to be so painfully upset. I think Robert felt really bad about his choice. He'd been asked to give things that would bring out a reaction in the kids— and boy, did he ever!

Kirk, too, had a joke aired on *TV's Bloopers and Practical Jokes*. The crew of *Growing Pains* had always threatened to get Kirk back for the endless jokes he'd played on them—and they were true to their word. Payback time came when Kirk had an appointment to get his car serviced and the crew knew about it. They contacted the dealership and had the service rep call Kirk and tell him that his car had been stolen off the lot. Kirk, stunned and horrified at this shocking news, handed the phone to me so I could get the information while Kirk paced the set in front of me.

Not much later, we received a call that they had "found" his car. I took Kirk to the impound lot to pick it up. When they brought out his white Honda Prelude hatchback hanging by a chain off the end of a tow truck, there was nothing left except the pitiful body frame. Kirk's mouth dropped open, his eyes wide as he went to what used to be his car. He walked around it and read the VIN number on the inside of the door frame. He came to me and said, "Mom, this isn't my car. I think they're trying to pull a fast one on us." He had memorized his vehicle ID with seventeen letters and numbers! At that moment, his Prelude pulled up alongside us filled with Robert, Melissa, Bridgette, and Candace hanging out of the sunroof. They all yelled, "You're on *TV's Bloopers and Practical Jokes!*" He was shocked. You could see the wheels in his head spinning, trying to figure out what had happened and started piecing together all the events from that day. He had been had!

For nine years of our lives, we had it all—the fame and lifestyle that so many try to achieve, and most only dream about. We couldn't know that lurking beneath the wave of excitement lay dangers that could steal our lives.

chapter 15

Fame

Fame brings with it an element to your lifestyle that you may not expect—or like. But if you become famous, you don't have much choice about it.

Fans.

Fans are critical to an actor's continued success. The more people an actor has wanting to see everything he stars in, the more jobs he can get. Actors love to act, and without acting jobs, they can't do what they love most. So fans are very important. Studios know that having Julia Roberts star in a movie will have far more people flocking to see it than if it starred some plain Jane no one has ever heard of. The more fans Kirk and Candace had, the more the series would be watched, and the longer the series would continue. Having a solid fan base keeps actors working at what they love.

My kids knew this, and they loved their fans, and so did I—until they became so unwieldy, we didn't know what to do.

Every time we went out to eat, people mobbed Kirk and Candace, wanting autographs. When we could, we asked for a booth, with Robert and me flanking the ends to keep people as far away from the kids as possible. Still, no matter where we were in the process of eating, people came up to ask for autographs, shoving napkins, papers, even bare hands over to be signed. The fans wanted Kirk more than Candace. Eventually, Kirk learned to say, "I'd be happy to sign as many autographs as you like—after I finish my meal." Most folks were understanding and polite, but some countered with rude, nasty comments.

To some extent, the kids liked being recognized and noticed. After all, who doesn't want to be liked when you're a teenager?

We attempted to go to Disneyland as a family, with Kirk disguised in sunglasses and a sport cap. But the fans instantly knew that curly hair and mobbed him. Another time, the studios invited the family to come to Magic Mountain, an amusement park in Southern California. After shooting a scene, Kirk and the family tried to have a normal visit to a park. The fans picked up pretty quickly that a curly headed teen being escorted by security was their beloved Mike Seaver. Some fan managed to snip off a lock of his hair for a souvenir!

On a number of trips to Hawaii, Kirk traveled under the pseudonym of Dale Olson and wore a false mustache, and sunglasses and hid his hair under a hat. The first time he did this, he called me from Kauai, delighted that no one had recognized him during his travel.

However, he couldn't be incognito all the time. So while in Hawaii, for example, while shopping at a store, resting on the beach, taking a walk, or even going on a tour, people followed him, mouths agape, asking for autographs and pictures. Kirk always answered graciously—but it made for a rather disconnected trip with his friends or family.

The tabloids only infuriated me. If they got anything right, that was unusual. Once the thing they got right made Kirk's life unsafe. They printed the make and the license plate number of his car. Soon after, someone tried to run Kirk off the freeway as he headed home from work. As you can imagine, this frightened him terribly.

The girl fans, especially, could present interesting situations. One girl, after waiting for hours to meet Kirk, stepped up to meet him on a stage, fainted, fell off, and broke her arm.

One time as we were leaving a car show in a limo, Kirk decided he'd throw rose petals—that a girl had just pressed into his hand—out the limo window. Suddenly grasping, wiggling fingers and eager hands were reaching into the car. I tried rolling up the window quickly and got Kirk's arm stuck. We all laughed, but should have learned our lesson!

At the "Say No to Drugs" parade in Chicago, Kirk and Tracey Gold were in a tower, and there were hundreds of girls below them. They were able to get Tracey down, but they couldn't get Kirk down from the tower because these girls were grabbing his feet. A strapping security guard told Bridgette and me to get inside the limo and wait for Kirk. "We're going to have to rush him," the guard explained. Bridgette and I huddled inside, screams of the girls outside only slightly muffled. Moments later, the door flies open, Kirk is thrown in by the guard, and the door slams shut. The limo driver had been ready to take off, but couldn't move because there were girls everywhere, swarming over the car. The driver leaned out of the car and started screaming, "Get out of the way!" Bridgette leaned into me, scared. The fans pounded on the window screaming, "Kirk, Kirk, Kirk. We love you, Kirk!"

If there was ever any doubt that Kirk had a huge fan base, the mail proved differently. Early on, Kirk started getting mail—5,000 letters a month. That soon escalated to 10,000 letters a month and more, until we stopped counting.

At first, we tried to read every letter and answer each one specially. I really had a heart to write back to these children who so desperately wanted to connect with Kirk in some way. In the beginning, when the mail arrived only a few letters at a time, I would open each one, read it, and respond with a picture postcard.

When the trickle turned into a landslide of paper pouring into our house, we knew we couldn't do it all alone. This was so overwhelming for us. We tried to figure out the most cost-effective way to respond. Big, 8 by 10 glossy, black-and-white pictures would have cost too much. We couldn't handwrite a personal response to every letter anymore, there were just too many coming in! So we decided to set up a fan club for Kirk. There were companies out there that would do this for us, but I felt that it just wasn't personal enough. I felt that these children put their hearts into these letters, and even shared their dreams and struggles. The right thing to do was to respond back to them in some way.

The fan club was organized in the building behind our home. Years before, Robert built a four-car garage, with two additional rooms, one of which we knew would be Robert's music room where he could practice his trumpet. This building extended across the back of our property. And Robert's hoped-for music room became the fan club headquarters.

My mother, sisters, Bridgette, Melissa, and Candace all helped out. We bought a button machine to make photo buttons of Kirk to include in the fan club kit we'd designed. Fans who'd join that would receive a folder of pictures of Kirk, a poster, Kirk Cameron button, and a letter from Kirk thanking them for their support. We also had a separate branch of the fan club where the fans could purchase different items like T-shirts. We even had a pillowcase with Kirk's picture on it! I can't believe we did that, but at the time it was one of our best sellers. I guess girls loved to sigh as they fell asleep, their face so close to Kirk's.

The sales of this merchandise helped offset the cost of mailing just the letters—without the fan club kit.

What we had hoped would be a fun business for the family turned into a business that was so large we couldn't do it anymore. As much as we wanted to respond to these children, we couldn't answer all of them. After a few years of doing the fan club, we decided to find a group of people to help us handle these letters. We went to our church and found a group of women who would open the mail and pick out the most touching letters to respond to. It broke my heart that we couldn't respond to each of them anymore, but it just wasn't possible. On occasion, I would receive letters about a serious situation, and I would have Kirk call the child on the phone, or I would send flowers to the child from Kirk. These acts of love were well received, and the parents would thank us so much for putting a smile on their child's face. I even have a poem that a woman named Bevy wrote for me. It was such an incredible poem that I tucked it inside my wallet and have never taken it out.

The paparazzi exist to support the fans—to have a juicy meal ready for their next feeding frenzy. When they did their job without going to extremes, it wasn't too bad. But sometimes, they could be terribly annoying.

Warner Brothers put on a special event, and Kirk spent a good deal of time interacting with the people there. When he was done, he tried to get away, riding a bike while wearing a hat, a goofy jacket, and big sunglasses. He couldn't lose the paparazzi, so Robert took

Barb's mom and her friend, Mrs. Marquez, helping in the Kirk Cameron Fan Club office.

him aside, and they exchanged clothes. Kirk hid, and Robert rode around on the bicycle, pretending to be Kirk. The paparazzi chased the decoy until he stopped and took off the disguise. Robert says he was very hurt that they were disappointed in who they saw.

Most fans were kind and respectful—even if carried away by their excitement sometimes. Others, if they didn't get what they wanted the moment they wanted it, were rude. But then, there was a whole other class of fans that I didn't know existed—or didn't want to believe existed.

A person more devious than most shattered our sense of safety.

This young man, a fan who "befriended" Jeremy Miller (Ben), got onto the set with tickets Jeremy had given him. He told us his brother, who lived in Canada, had cancer and was a big fan of Kirk's. "May I get a picture with Kirk to send to my brother? It would mean so much to him."

We readily agreed, and I ran around trying to find someone with a camera, when the young man produced his own. We took the picture. The result probably made it look as though Kirk and this young man were friends.

A few months later, this young man showed up on our doorstep with a young boy by his side. "We'd like to see Kirk," he said.

"I'm sorry he's not here," I told them. I couldn't quite place where I'd seen him before, not remembering the brief visit on the set. After all, I met fans every week on tape night. Both of them seemed a little nervous, and something about them made me uneasy.

"Can I have his phone number?" the young man asked, his voice sounding forced.

"Let me get a pencil and paper. I'll take your number, and Kirk can call you later." I left the door wide open, and found my pad and paper where I always left it by the phone. He wrote his number on it, and left with the young boy.

A couple of weeks later, I got a call at home from the police department. They wanted to talk with Kirk, but he wasn't at home at the time. I asked if they would let me know what was going on, and they said that they needed to talk with him about a situation that had occurred. I told them that they could meet Kirk and me on the set the next day. When they arrived, we invited them into Kirk's trailer.

The police had to ask Kirk questions about a man, probing to know who he was. Kirk and I were both confused, not having any idea who they were talking about.

The policeman showed us a picture of Kirk and the man in question. I instantly recognized it as the one that I had taken. It was blown up into an 8 by 10—not unusual for a fan to do.

"Mrs. Cameron," the policeman began. "This man has been using this photograph as a lure."

"I don't understand."

"He shows this photograph to young boys, telling them he's Kirk's friend. Then he asks if they want to go to the studio and meet him."

Kirk didn't move. I felt the blood drain from my face.

"He has been successful in attracting at least one young boy into his car. He then molested him."

I felt sick. And frightened. This person had been to my door! He knew where we lived! A cold shiver went up my spine. I had turned my back on him, leaving our door open!

"The young boy escaped and told us that he had seen a picture of this guy and Kirk Cameron."

"I'm sorry," I said. "I'm so terribly sorry. We don't know who he is."

Kirk spoke up. "I remember he drives a really hot car."

"He told us his brother is in Canada, dying of cancer. We took the picture to give to him."

"We'd like to get him, Mrs. Cameron, and we'd like Kirk to help."

I couldn't believe it. I didn't want my son anywhere near this man.

The officer must have correctly read the look on my face. "I don't know that we can get him unless we use Kirk."

"I'll have to talk to my husband."

Later that evening, Robert and I discussed the situation. We called a friend of ours who was a detective for another police department. He advised us against using our young son as a decoy to trap a criminal. We were relieved to have our own preferences confirmed.

The police weren't thrilled with our decision, but managed to make a plan that only remotely used us. They set up a fictitious phone number that Jeremy gave the next time the young man called him.

"You want to come to see a taping of the show?" Jeremy asked him. The guy was delighted, and Jeremy told him the fictitious time to appear, and through which gate to enter the lot.

On the specified day, undercover cops dressed as groundskeepers, studio security, and ordinary people scattered about the area where the young man should appear. He drove through the assigned gate in his hot car, and the "security" directed him to a particular parking spot. Once he shut the engine off, police appeared from everywhere, guns drawn, shouting at him. "GET DOWN ON THE GROUND! GET DOWN *NOW*. PLACE YOUR HANDS ON THE BACK OF YOUR HEAD!"

"I DIDN'T DO ANYTHING!" he protested. "What's this all about?"

"You have the right to remain silent. Anything you say can and will be used against you in a court of law."

Inside the soundstage, someone yelled, "It's a sting! The cops have someone!"

Relief flooded through me. They'd gotten him.

Unfortunately, that wasn't the only situation. In another, someone had shown up at Kirk's high school (where he was enrolled, but didn't attend) and said they had a motorcycle as a thank-you gift for Kirk from the police. They wanted his address to deliver it.

Friends from Racquetball World called to let Robert know someone had been asking a lot of questions about Kirk and seemed to be stalking him.

Fans sometimes showed up in our backyard, having read that Kirk lived in the converted garage behind the house.

"This has to stop!" I told Robert.

He didn't hesitate to take necessary steps to protect his family. We had an armored car pick up Kirk daily from the house for a short time, and return him to us until we were certain the danger was over. We had motion-detector lights put on around the house. And we had an electric security gate installed around the house. No one could even get to the front door without permission. We turned over all suspicious and threatening letters to detectives (but didn't tell Kirk about them). We didn't want to scare Kirk, but we did want him to be cautious.

And then we discovered our accountant had stolen an extremely large amount of money from us. He had been purchasing cars, vacations, even a boat—all with money embezzled from the accounts of our children. We were stunned, betrayed. This man had been a trusted family friend! We had trusted him with everything. And he had calmly, coolly, and casually taken money that we would never recover.

These instances shook my foundation. What had I done to my kids? I never thought these things could ever happen to us. But they did. I beat myself up—why didn't I see them coming? Was our life so out of my control? I thought this was supposed to be fun, exciting, and glamorous. Had I put my children in danger? Had I only thought about myself and what I want? Where did I go wrong? Is this the price of fame? How did we get here, and who do I trust?

chapter 16

Finally, Love

When I was a little girl, body-surfing in the ocean sometimes brought danger. The waves, if caught at the wrong time, or tinged with an undertow, could suck me under. Fighting the water didn't do any good. The unseen forces punched me this way and that, tugging me under, rolling me into flaying somersaults, and then pulling me backward instead of spitting me out on the beach. My heart thumped in terror, my mind spinning prayers to God, hoping He could hear me even if I was underwater.

Eventually, I'd be safe on land. Like when I was at my Aunt June's pool, slipping further and further into the deep end when something lifted me so I could hold onto the side and be safe. Secure once more.

Living with Robert, with continual fear that what I said or did might cause an argument, sucked me under like a riptide. Being tossed about and slammed down, not being able to breathe while I tried to scramble to my feet, I fought for air until I thought my heart would give out. The effort to simply exist was overwhelming. Prayers, attempting to talk to Robert, fighting, clamming up—nothing worked. My feet slipped on the slippery slope to where I knew soon I would drown.

With every waking breath, I prayed for relief.

Relief, the safety of shore, handholds on the side of the pool, came every Thursday and Friday in the sparkling eyes, welcoming smile, and tenderness of a crew member named Steve. His very presence stopped the undertow. Each week I looked for this relief, longed for it, yearned for it. Every time Steve was around, the pull was gone, and I felt like I could get on my feet again. I discovered that when I leaned on him, I found some rest for my weary, broken heart. Each time, I leaned just a little bit more, just a little bit harder for more rest, more reassurance. It felt so good to be away from that chaos of undertow.

So on Wednesday nights my mind thought ahead. I couldn't wait for Thursday. Couldn't wait to see him and talk to him. To bask in the warmth of relief. Just the anticipation of seeing him filled me with a giddy excitement that I had to suppress. I thought of all sorts of shrewd ways to get a chance to talk to him, to just be close to him.

In the beginning, I observed him like any other crew member. His friendly spirit surrounded him like a happy cloud, and I wanted to be inside that whenever I could. Within time, I began to notice I was attracted on a deeper level to his gentleness and laughter. Each day I saw him, I wanted to be around him more and more. I had a sense of being full, alive, and safe—just how I'd always dreamed life was supposed to be.

During the early days, I did not intend to walk away from my marriage. I planned to be good and moral and do what was right—stay with my marriage—no matter how difficult it got, even if it succeeded in draining out my last breath of self, becoming a lifeless person.

There were days when I looked at the marriage honestly, realizing it (and I) wouldn't last if the relationship continued on as it was. On those days I entertained thoughts of ending it when Candace turned eighteen.

When I contemplated how wrong divorce was, I'd swing back to the other side, to the fact that I wanted very much to do things the right way. I'd be solid in that thinking until Robert and I had another fight. The frustration of it all swept over me, and I'd think only about leaving again.

Nursing the anticipation that I'd soon see Steve on the set swelled within me, a delighted joy I hadn't experienced continually from the presence of a man since Robert and I had first dated. Steve had crew jobs in other places as well as *Growing Pains*, and so I'd see him only those two days a week. Those days became the best of my week as I talked with him, and had lunch and dinner with him on the set.

Fridays, on tape night, I'd dress up very nice, hoping to catch his eye more.

"Why are you so dressed up?" Robert would ask.

To escape the riptide.

"I'm Kirk's mother," I said. "I should look nice." I hoped he wouldn't see through the lie to the truth. I also hoped he would choose *not* to come to the taping. He'd begun to come more and more often so we could all be together as a family. I wanted him to stay away like he used to. I wanted the chance to be around Steve without having to worry that Robert might see the change in me.

Around Steve, I felt something flutter to life that I thought had died long ago. The yearning to be appreciated was finally satisfied and disappeared when Steve spent time with me. Worth and respect, values I continually wanted to instill inside my children toward all human beings, came pouring from Steve into me. Robert lived and preached those values as well, but did not give them to the one person closest to him.

In time I knew. In Steve, at last, was my chance to be truly loved. Someone had lifted me, placing my hands on the side of the pool. But I was torn between wanting to be loved and cherished, and wanting to be the good wife.

I didn't know what to do. At first, I thought it was harmless to spend time with Steve. We weren't doing anything wrong—just talking. Yet, like grains of sand eventually becoming a beach, each moment spent talking with Steve eventually evolved into something more than just friendship. I moved to flirting. I leaned and leaned, until I leaned too far.

I don't know when I crossed the line in my heart. I certainly wasn't consciously aware of it. Honestly, I would have been horrified had I paid attention. The affection and attraction for Steve grew in such small increments that I didn't realize they were there until they were so huge, I couldn't deny them anymore. I was caught up in a new current—one that lightened my heavy spirit, refreshed, nourished. I didn't really care where this current might take me. It could only be good.

On the way home from work on Thursdays, I felt alternately full of joy and incredible sadness. Instead of turning away from thoughts I shouldn't be entertaining, I tore at what good there was in my marriage. Why couldn't Robert pour into me the way Steve did? Why did my marriage have to be so miserable? Why couldn't I have the tenderness Steve exuded, rather than the harsh, brash, hurtful words of Robert?

I tried to think how I contributed to the misery of the marriage. But it all seemed so mixed together that I couldn't tell where one person's actions or words began, and the other's ended. Everything seemed to be circling into itself.

I soon realized I had everything I wanted on the outside, and had nothing on the inside. I had been true to the good little girl inside me, yet I felt empty.

When my thoughts turned to Robert, more and more I saw only the negative. I never felt like we were "one" in our marriage. The qualities that I liked about Robert when I married him were the things that I now disliked about him—his overpowering strength and his loud, forceful opinions. I'd heard all his jokes and no longer laughed at them. They bored me.

I had finally come into my own as a manager, as a woman. I had my own money. I had the confidence I'd lacked before. I had my own opinions now about many things—things Robert didn't necessarily have a working knowledge of, like the complicated business of television and movie acting. However, whenever I tried to express any thought or opinion to Robert, I would be shot down. His tone was harsh and intimidating. If I expressed opinions to Steve, he considered them and discussed them as coming from an intelligent person. He knew the world I now moved around in. And he cared about it. He knew its complications and the ramifications of small actions.

Robert still held everything about the business with a hint of disdain. He had no idea what it took for our kids to make it through a day. He had no idea how hard those kids worked, and how respected they were by others much older than they. I grieved that Robert refused to join us in our world, to be a part of it—or, at the very least, to respect it.

Steve gave me everything Robert didn't. He gave me encouragement not only as a woman and a manager, but also as a person. He provided thoughtful feedback to my questions and opinions. He treated me as someone special. I can't say enough how that poured through my entire being to the point of bringing tears of gratitude on many occasions. I thanked God for bringing this angel into my life.

Steve also brought much laughter and fun. He liked to play practical jokes, sometimes getting Kirk back for the ones played on him. Watching him tease the other actors and crew, bringing a light-hearted spirit to the environment, drew me ever closer to him.

I became so obsessed with Steve that I began thinking of any possible way to be with him. I let my mind go to places it didn't belong. I lost weight, and found myself buying new clothes to wear on tape nights—just for him. I was very good at not letting anyone know about what was going on inside me. Even though we exchanged a kiss on the lips when we saw each other, I also kissed others on the lips as well. (Kissing is very much a part of life in Hollywood circles.) I sensed that when Steve kissed me, there was more to it than anyone else would notice.

Around Steve, I felt attractive, desired. The chemistry sparked between us, lighting me and making me crave more. And then I would go home where it seemed Robert didn't care for my body shape and type. Why had he married me if he didn't care for what I had? I didn't understand.

I began going to a counselor to try to make sense of my mixed-up thoughts and feelings. I didn't tell her about Steve. I didn't tell anyone about him. I kept it all tucked away inside a neat and tidy little box that held every memory of every moment with him.

An internal voice began to speak positive words to me. Instead of always thinking of the negative about Robert, I began to embrace the idea of divorce. The more I thought about it, the more I heard inside my head, *You can do this; it's okay. You'll be better off. The kids will be fine. They'll adjust. You're the strong one now; Robert's the weak one. You can handle it. You go get that apartment you wanted so long ago—the one you never got to have. Go be independent like you always wanted to be. You went from being under your parents' rule immediately to under Robert's. Now's YOUR chance. Go experience all those things that you always wanted. Go experience having a relationship with someone else. You deserve better than what you have right now. You deserve it. Life is better than what you're living. Life is fun. You should be happy.*

My thoughts mingled and tore at each other. My stomach hurt while I tried to decide what to do. Everything I'd ever known and believed in seemed to be on one side of the fence or the other. Either I could be good, or I could be loved. I couldn't have both.

I fought with myself on every level. I wanted both, believed I could have both, but when it came down to it, I had to make a choice.

I talked for hours with the counselor, who encouraged me to break free from Robert to make a new start.

It all sounded so wonderful.

And beckoning to me from the other side stood a man with deep blue eyes and a fabulous smile.

I could do this.

"I'd like to meet with you," I whispered to Steve one day.

He cocked his head, fork holding potato salad stopped midway between his plate and his mouth. "What do you mean?"

"Away from here." I smiled, hoping he could read what I couldn't say there, where other ears might hear.

It took him a moment. And then he said, "Monday. Santa Monica beach. Do you know where the little coffee shop is near the pier?"

"Sure."

"At two?"

"Okay."

Monday, I sent the girls to their friends and made sure Robert hadn't gotten off work early. I dressed in my blue slacks and white jacket. I knew I looked hot. I got in my silver BMW and took off for the beach, my heart pounding with anticipation. The whole way there, I practiced what I would say, and dreamed about our first real kiss. I couldn't wait to be tucked under his arm, my head leaning on his chest.

I pulled into the driveway of the coffee shop and found a parking spot. Steve walked up to the car and opened the door for me to get out.

"Do you want to walk?" he asked.

"Yes," I said, all my practiced words having vanished from my brain.

We walked without saying much. Both of us were probably dancing around the huge issue between us. A cool breeze lifted my long, blond hair and swirled it around my face. I pushed away the strands and tried to tuck them behind my ears. I wanted him to take my hand—and he did. We walked along the beach, and then sat in the sand, close to the water. He put his arm around me, and I snuggled into that crook of safety and affection. I leaned my head against his chest, knowing I'd found where I needed to be.

We sat without speaking for a while, letting the waves come to us, then running away, leaving hissing foam behind.

"Did you want to talk about something?" Steve asked.

I nodded. "I wanted to tell you that, well, first of all, I miss you when I don't see you. I'm so glad we can finally be alone." I took a breath, afraid, but determined to tell him more. "I really care about you."

"I care about you a lot, Barb." He sounded sincere, but something else I couldn't pinpoint lay behind his words.

I looked out at the sea, instead of at him, trying to gather the words that seemed to be scattering faster than I could put them together. "It's that, well ..." I sighed and picked up his hand, playing with it. "You are an amazing man, Steve." And then the words came together and poured out, gushing like a broken dam. "I wanted to have the chance to talk about how I feel about you. I'm falling for you, and want to spend more time with you—away from the set. I know I'm married, but my marriage isn't good. He treats me so badly. He says horrible things to me all the time."

I let go of his hand and drew in the sand, telling him some of the stories about Robert. I could sense him looking at me. I looked up into eyes that seemed filled with pain. I kept going. "My children really like you, and I know you care for them. That would make things a lot easier for all of us."

His pained look didn't change. It threw me a bit, but I finished my little speech. "Since meeting you and spending time with you, I realize how much I'm missing in my life. I want to be with you."

Steve tenderly put his fingers to my mouth, and looked deeply into my eyes. "Shhh."

My heart leapt in hope. I waited expectantly.

"I can't have a relationship with you, Barb."

An unseen fist slammed into my stomach.

"I respect you too much. I respect your marriage. And I could never, ever hurt your kids that way."

"My marriage is over," I pleaded.

Steve shook his head. "I will not be the reason a marriage ended."

"I want us to be together."

"We can't."

"Why?" I said, with a million other unspoken "whys" trailing behind the first.

He took a deep breath. "I don't care for you in the same way that you care about me, Barb."

I looked at his face, searched for the lie I knew had to be displayed there. "You do. I've seen it on the set day after day. I've sensed in the way you look at me, the way you talk to me."

Steve took his arm from my shoulder and looked down at his feet, his hands dangling between his bent knees.

"Tell me the truth," I said, trying not to shiver with the shattering of my dreams.

"The truth is, we can't be together."

"Why?"

"I told you, Barb. I respect and value you too much to do this to you, to your kids, to your marriage."

I held in my tears, frantically trying to come up with a new plan.

Steve stood, offering me his hand. I took it, and we walked some more.

A big red sign read *No Lifeguard On Duty*. I walked with Steve to the ramp that led up to the little lifeguard lookout perched on spindly legs. We sat in the doorway of the lookout, watching the waves crash rhythmically against the shore. Few people were hardy enough to sunbathe in the brisk temperatures. The sun felt warm, but the breeze blew cool. When a cloud hid the sun, I could almost shiver.

I looked up at Steve and moved in to kiss him, knowing that would bring out the truth—and his desire for me. He kissed back, but not as enthusiastically as I had dreamed. We kissed a little more, but I felt something wasn't right. Was he holding back? Where was the unleashed passion? Was I not pretty enough? Not skinny enough? What was wrong with me? Did I kiss that bad?

He pulled back. "Come on, Barb. Let's go."

He again took my hand and helped me up, and led me down the ramp, then let go of my hand.

All that I had dreamed spilled away. We walked back to the coffee shop and our cars in silence, not touching. At my car, Steve opened the door. He took both my hands in his. "I will always care about you, Barb."

I looked away, not able to stand the pain of seeing him and knowing that he didn't want me. Then, the cloud of restrained tears let loose a downpour. Steve pulled me in to his chest. I sobbed, my tears staining his shirt.

On the drive home, I kept thinking about the conversation, running it over and over through my head. The thing was, I knew Steve had to be lying. I may have been sheltered, but I knew how men look at women they care for. And Steve did not look at other women he worked with the same way he looked at me. He did not treat others the same way he treated me.

I knew his words weren't true.

The nearer I got to home, the more I realized that I had choices that would lead me closer to Steve. I *could* divorce Robert. I *could* be free of him. Then Steve would see that he wasn't the cause of a marriage dying—that it had died before he had come into the picture. He would see what a strong woman I am, a woman worthy of being desired, pursued, and loved. My dream wasn't yet dead. I would not let the man of my dreams get away. I would do whatever I could to make this work—even if that meant leaving Robert.

chapter 17

On My Own

I have nothing.

Unless you count an empty, ugly marriage.

And the man I thought would give me at least a chance for love said, "No."

I have nothing.

I cried all day. When Robert asked why, I told him to go away.

Thursday, instead of being the best day of the week, became the worst. It tore my heart out to see Steve. To not be able to eat with him, talk with him, hug him. After the first painful day, if I didn't have to go to the set, I didn't. I still went to tape nights. I still dressed up. I still hoped. I still dreamed.

A month crawled by. Then two.

I realized that I would have to fight ... I would have to fight for my marriage, or I'd have to fight for a chance at a relationship with Steve.

I *had* fought for my marriage. Anyone else would have given up the battle long ago. If I chose my marriage, wouldn't I die? I was already near death emotionally.

If I chose Steve, I would have the joy of life, of living and walking tall rather than hiding in the shadows.

I chose to fight for Steve.

My counselor, without telling me what to do, encouraged me to leave. That day I left my counseling appointment and headed home. It didn't take long after I arrived for Robert to say something in that tone I disliked. All my frustration exploded out of all the places I'd been hiding them. I clenched my fists, stood as tall as I could, and screamed, "I'm leaving you! I've had enough!"

I fled into the bedroom and began yanking open drawers and pulling clothes out. I threw them on the bed. The pile of my necessities grew as I threw on items from the closet, the bathroom. I yanked the largest suitcases I had off the top shelf of the closet and crammed the piles into them.

"Come on, Barb, don't do this," Robert said. He looked stunned. But not like he really believed me.

"I want a divorce," I said. "I've had enough of your abuse. I'm not going to listen to you shred me anymore." Another wad of stuff went into the suitcase.

"You aren't serious, are you?" Robert pleaded, looking smaller and smaller.

I paused, the lid of the suitcase ready to close on my essential things. "I should have done this years ago. I am a *person*, Robert. I am a good woman and a good wife, and I deserve far more than you have ever given me."

I picked up the two suitcases and dragged them into the living room. Robert began to cry. "Please don't go, Barbara. I love you."

That did it. *Love? Did he say love?* I shook my head, opened the front door, and bumped the suitcases down the stairs to the BMW. I heaved them into the trunk, slammed it, and drove off.

I found a Vagabond Hotel just down the road, and checked in. I opened the suitcase and carefully put away all my things, then sat at the small table, wondering what I should do next.

Calming down, I knew my next step needed to be to tell Robert where I was. After all, I was still the manager of the kids' careers. Kirk had moved out of the house to the apartment Robert had converted from the garage out back, next to the fan club. Kirk could get himself to and from work, but still needed me to manage. Candace would need to be picked up daily and taken to work. And most of all, I wanted my kids to know where I was so they could reach me if they needed to.

"Robert?" I said on the phone, keeping my voice firm. "We need to talk."

"Okay," came the voice so weak. I could hear tears beginning to rise to the surface of it. I had rarely seen Robert cry in our seventeen years of marriage. I suppose I should have been softened by tears, but I realized my subconscious had been working on leaving him for quite some time. My days of grieving about this were over.

"We need to tell the kids something," I directed.

"Okay. When? How?"

"The sooner the better, don't you think?"

"Yes," he said, trying to speak through his tears.

We talked a bit more, and I drove home and picked up Bridgette, taking her to the grocery store with me to buy things for dinner. I tried to act very chatty and upbeat, but she saw through my act. When we got back to the car she asked, "Are you and Daddy all right?"

The question came so unexpectedly that it got around my guard, and I put my head on the steering wheel and started to sob. After a moment, I stopped the flow of tears and reached for a tissue. I took Bridgette's hand. "Daddy and I are going through some tough stuff."

"Are you getting a divorce?"

"No," I said, "but we're going to separate for a while."

Thankfully, Bridgette didn't ask any more questions as we drove home. She watched me, though, observing me as if my face might tell her more.

At home, we put away the groceries and cooked dinner. Robert and I didn't look at each other. He barely touched his food.

Afterwards, we gathered the three oldest in the living room, feeling that Candace, at twelve, was too young for the conversation. "We have something to tell you," I began gently, softly. I reached out my hand and took Melissa's hand on one side and Kirk's on the other. They instinctively reached for the hand next to them. We sat there in a circle, tears streaming down Robert's face. The kids alternately looked from his melting face to my hardened one. "Daddy and I are having some trouble," I said. "We're going to separate for a little while to see if we can work things out."

"Are you going to get a divorce?" Melissa asked.

Robert looked at me, hopeful.

"We're going to separate," I repeated. "I am going to get an apartment really close by. Things won't change much. I just won't be sleeping here."

A dark cloud settled on Melissa. She took her hand away from mine and wrapped it around her waist. Her glare told me all I needed to know about how she felt about it.

I drove back to the hotel, convinced the kids would be fine. They were good kids. Their father needed them.

Within a week, I found an apartment, rented furniture, got a phone line, and moved in. We decided that Candace should come live with me to make it easier for her to get up and ready in the morning since the other girls needed to leave for school earlier than Candace had to go to work. We fixed it up very cute, and brought Bridgette and Melissa to show it off.

"Yeah, Mom, it's cute," Melissa said, but she still glowered at me and grumbled as she spoke.

"When are you and Dad getting back together?" Bridgette asked.

"I don't know."

All my life I had never lied to my kids. I always gave them the straight talk about whatever it was I needed to say. Sometimes our conversations made me uncomfortable, but I always told them what I thought and felt, even if it was unpopular and made them angry with me for being so close-minded or prudish. So it felt weird to lie to them. I didn't like it, but I felt it necessary. Until we made the decisions that would be more final, I felt it better to let them believe in their hearts what they wanted to believe.

The separation continued to be very difficult on Robert. For me, I felt relieved, finally free. I felt total peace that I had made the right decision. I made sure Steve had my phone number, almost giddy when I gave it to him. Now he would see that I was serious about my marriage being intolerable. Now he would see that *he* was not the cause of our marriage ending. It was doomed anyway—with or without Steve.

Every evening I stared at the phone, willing for it to ring. It seemed as though my heart had hands, reaching for Steve through the phone, wanting him to realize that he was lying to himself. Of course, he cared about me. I could see it even on those painful Thursdays. Why wouldn't he give in to it?

And then, the perfect opportunity to encourage Steve and me to get together landed right in my lap.

The producer informed me that *Growing Pains* planned to go to Maui, Hawaii, to film a show. We'd stay at the brand new, very elegant resort hotel, Makena Prince. The set buzzed with excitement, and new hope opened inside me. *Here's my chance.*

In the months we had to wait until the preparations had been made by location scouts, managers, producers, I casually told Robert he didn't need to go. We needed him at home to take care of the girls. Someone had to go with Kirk, and it made more sense for me to go. Really, it was okay for me to manage Kirk alone.

Renewed and revitalized daydreams swam through my thought life. I could picture myself as thin, tan, looking great on the beach. Steve would look out his hotel room window and see me. He wouldn't be able to resist coming to talk to me. I wouldn't be forward, but I would be enticing. I'd flirt a little, letting him move closer. He'd invite me to dinner—alone. I'd accept. Walks on the beach at sunset. And then? Well, my thoughts were *not* rated G.

It didn't take a long time in this industry to know that affairs and new relationships happened on location all the time. The exotic locales, the intense time working and playing together, eating great food at someone else's expense, staying in romantic hotels or hideaways—everything played into romance embracing two people in its warm energy. If new romance was a commonplace on-location occurrence, then I intended to become one of the fortunate victims.

I bought new clothes and stashed them away, not wanting Candace to see them. I took great care to keep my slim figure at a size 8, wanting to look drop-dead gorgeous in the new swimsuits I had hidden in the back of my closet. I grew more brave in talking with Steve on the set again. I dressed nicely both days. Soon, it was almost as though we had not had that day on the beach.

By the time we landed in Maui, I couldn't have been more excited. I unpacked in my private room, threw open the sliding doors, and leaned on my balcony railing. The warm, flower-scented breeze lifted my hair gently from my shoulders. I touched the fresh lei around my neck, and decided to change into something more casual. I put on a tiny sundress, slipped on sandals, freshened up my makeup, and went out to explore the hotel and beach.

I punched the elevator button. When the doors slid open, there stood Steve! My heart leapt. And then I saw *her*. His arm around her shoulder. "Barbara," Steve said, forcing a smile, "I'd like you to meet Laura."

I also forced a smile and shook her hand as all my joy, my delight, my plans, and my fantasies vanished. Crushed, I turned to look at the numbers flashing over the door, hoping my tears would wait.

During the week we were there, I still tried to nurture hope. I walked along the beach at sunset, or sat where he might be able to catch a glimpse of me from a hotel room. I made myself obviously available, hoping that somehow he'd see that Laura wasn't who he really wanted.

I returned from Hawaii feeling miserable. Was I doomed to a life without love?

When I turned the key to my apartment, and flung open the door, the living room had fresh flowers, balloons, and crepe paper. "Happy Birthday, Mom" a banner read. Gifts sat on the coffee table. Something lifted in me. Robert would have had to go through some hoops to make this happen. Did he actually care? Were his tears for real? Was this his way of showing me that he wanted to make me feel special because I *was* special to him?

Yeah, right, I thought, the skeptic in me taking over. *How long is this going to last? If he's going to win me back, he has some serious changing to do.*

I had to be strong now. I couldn't let one sweet thing he did sway me. I put up my guard, determined to be very, very careful in taking my next step.

chapter 18

The Empty Room

At first, living on my own in the apartment was a blast. I loved coming home to my cute little place—the place I'd always dreamed of having. I enjoyed being able to do whatever I wanted, whenever I wanted to, and not worrying about stepping on a land mine what would cause an explosive reaction in my husband. It was nice not to have to continually wade through tension, palpable in my former home.

Yet after Hawaii, it seemed as though someone had rearranged the furniture in my mental house. Maybe the loss of hope cleared the air of fantasies that didn't belong there anyway. With all chance of a life with Steve—or even dating him—efficiently removed by *Laura*, I had nothing else to think about except what in the world I wanted to do with the rest of my life.

Managing my kids wouldn't last forever. They would grow up. The series would eventually end. And then what? I could open my own agency like I'd been dreaming about on occasion. But would that hold the satisfaction and completeness that I longed for? What about love and commitment?

Candace spent more time at home with her sisters. They missed her terribly and voiced their anger at their dad that their best friend had been taken away from them. The kids were not doing as well as I had supposed. Stoic Robert cried a lot. He told Melissa through his tears how much she looked like me, cleaned like me, cooked like me. He cried every day when dropping the girls off at school. He cried so hard, that sometimes he'd bang his head on the wall.

My own loneliness began to take up more room in the apartment than my delight at living by myself. I started to drop by the house more often, sometimes calling the girls out to the car to talk to them. I didn't feel welcome to just pop inside the house, of course. It wasn't my home anymore, and I didn't have a right to just walk in.

One day, as I pulled into the driveway, Robert came out to greet me. Standing at the passenger side of my car, he noticed a magazine lying on the front seat. Large print on the cover asked the question, "Are you a positive or negative person?"

"I'm a pretty positive guy," he blurted.

I stared at him. "You're kidding, right? You are the most negative person I've ever met!"

"No, I'm not. I'm very positive." He looked as though I'd whacked him with the broad side of a board, obviously shocked that I could see him that way.

Unbeknownst to me, Robert decided he would ask other people what they thought. "Negative" was the consensus. This startled Robert again and again. With all this outside input something clicked inside him, and he decided to do something about it. He started changing.

Little by little, I noticed small changes. The tone of voice he used when he spoke to me had lost the sharp points. It lacked the sarcasm. He looked at me with kind eyes, rather than narrowed eyes, or looking past me. His body language seemed to have lost the antagonism, replaced by a more normal stance that I'd seen him use with others. The girls revealed that Dad was treating them differently as well. I watched and waited to see if the changes were real and not just for show.

A friend invited Robert to his church. Robert, distressed and at the end of his rope, decided to go. "Okay, girls," he said one evening. "We're going somewhere."

"Where are we going, Dad?" Candace asked.

"Never mind. Just get ready."

The girls knew better than to ask more questions. Their father would not tell them and would only get angry. The four piled into the car, and drove to a large warehouse.

"Where are we?" the girls asked.

"Church."

The girls stared at each other, unable to comprehend this totally out-there thing their father had just done. Plus, this long, flat, ugly building did not look like any church they could imagine.

They all enjoyed it very much, and began to attend—all without telling me.

Around this same time, Kirk was dating a lovely girl whom he met when she had made a guest appearance on *Growing Pains*. They spent a lot of time together, and she talked with him about her belief in Jesus Christ. Then she invited Kirk to come to church with her. He decided that even he could go to church if it meant that he could spend a little more time with her.

But what he heard there shook his world. He heard about God and sin, he heard about how God viewed him, and it made him think. About a month later, as he dropped this girl off at acting lessons, he sat in his car, fully aware that he would die someday. And it might even be that day.

Kirk: I wondered what would happen if I died. Was there a heaven? Would I go there? It didn't take much to look around me and see that I had everything as a teenager that most people worked their entire lives for: money, fame, excitement, and travel. But even with all my success, if what I'd heard the pastor say was true, and there was a God and a heaven, I wouldn't be going there. I knew my attitude separated me from God, and there was no reason He should let me into heaven.

It really bothered me. I thought, maybe I'm wrong about this, I don't know. I decided to pray. I didn't know how to do it, but I closed my eyes. *God,* I prayed, *if You're there, I need to know. If You're real, would You please show me? And would You please forgive me and show me who You want me to be?*

I didn't see a vision of Jesus on the windshield; I didn't see the Holy Spirit rushing through the air vents, nothing weird. I just had this very strange sense that God was there, that He heard me, that He was listening to me. I can't prove it to you; I can't explain it, but it

was real. I went home. Someone gave me a Bible, and I began to
read.

Kirk didn't talk to me about his new faith. But I knew that he
spent a lot of time reading his Bible—even late into the night. He
began going to church, and I sensed it was no longer for a girl, but to
satisfy a hunger inside him. Kirk enjoyed talking with his girlfriend's
father, asking questions and seeking out what this new faith meant.
He attended their church, eating up everything he could.

At work, Kirk stopped joining in the more crass games and jokes
played on the set. He took his guitar and played worship songs while
sitting on the steps of his trailer. He opened the back part of his
hatchback and sat there as well, singing and playing.

Kirk, laughing: I was hoping someone would say, "Wow, do
you feel all that peace that passes understanding coming from the
back of that car? I want to know more about it."

He spent more time in his trailer, reading the Bible. He decided
to be a sort of modern-day scribe, and began writing the book of
Matthew by hand on pieces of parchment paper. He drew margins
and faint pencil lines, erasing them when he finished writing the text
in a neat calligraphy. "I want to write the entire Bible by hand for my
children," he told me.

Kirk had found direction and perspective on life through his new
relationship with God, but I still struggled in the place I'd created for
myself. My new home wasn't so fun anymore. This whole separation
thing wasn't going the way I'd planned. The apartment was cute, but
I missed my home. I missed that daily interaction with all my kids.

And the real shocker: I started missing Robert.

We had so many memories together. Lots of good ones, if I thought
about it. Robert would always give me a foot rub if I just put my foot
in his lap. Or he'd rub my back. I missed the joking around, our talks
over ice cream, the laughter, the conversations, and the family
gatherings. I missed the questions he asked people, getting them to
dive deeper and reveal more about themselves. He brought out the
extraordinary stories in seemingly ordinary people.

My heart opened a new door to a room that ached so much. I thought that room would be full of all the Hollywood happenings, my fun experiences with meeting exciting people, traveling to new places, having prestige. But those things didn't exist to inhabit *that* room. No, that room was for marriage and family. Nothing could replace those things.

But I couldn't go back to what had been. I couldn't subject myself to continual verbal battering. I refused to. Steve had done so many wonderful things for my spirit. I knew that better things existed and could be had in a relationship. I would not settle for an undertow when I'd experienced—if only for a moment—the delight of a stream.

One day, months after I had moved from home, the phone rang. I had ceased to believe it could be Steve. Only Robert or the kids ever called me here.

"Barb," Robert said, sounding quite happy. "Can you come stay with the kids tonight? I've got somewhere I need to go."

"Where are you going?"

There was a long pause. "That's information you don't need to know."

"Who are you going with?"

"A friend."

"What friend?" My heart started pounding. My stomach coiled into itself.

"That's information you don't need to know. Will you come?"

"Yes, I'll come."

I arrived a few minutes before the appointed time. I dropped my purse inside the living room and turned to see Robert looking quite handsome in a dark suit. "Wow," I said. "Just a simple evening with friends?" I hoped to trick him into telling me his plans.

Robert shrugged. He lifted an eyebrow at me and teased. "You think I look great, eh?"

My heart could have stopped. *This is the Robert I fell in love with.* "When will you be back?"

"I don't know. I'll call you." He winked. I died.

Heartsick, I watched him say good-bye to his girls. Did he think I didn't know he was going out on a date? How dare he! We were still *married*.

A double standard replaced logic in my brain.

I was the one who was supposed to be dating. *I* was the one who was supposed to be starting over—not *him.*

While the girls watched way too much television, I paced the floor, trying to figure out *who* he could have met. *Where* he could have met her.

I tried to remind myself that I'd always known that if something happened to me, he would marry quickly—and she'd probably have a great figure. It wouldn't happen fast out of disloyalty, but he was the kind of man who needed a woman.

But then the image of a gorgeous woman with great cleavage haunted me.

My own loneliness and a new jealousy joined hands and filled me with despair. I don't know that I had ever experienced such incredible agony. I slammed the bedroom door, then found items to heave against the wall in my fury. I dropped myself on the bed, sobbing, pounding the bed, all the drama of Hollywood right here in my own—I mean former—bedroom.

Would he bring her here someday?

My chest ached from the sobs rolling through it. My throat felt raw. My heart torn open with the truth—I loved Robert. I didn't love the awful way he treated me, but I loved who he was. He had never said no to anything new I wanted to try or do. As much as he thought Hollywood foolish, he didn't say no, allowing the kids adventures, relationships, and financial freedom that most adults never get to experience. Without him taking up the load at home, the kids and I would never have been able to work. He *never, ever* demanded a meal, or that the house be clean, or the clothes washed. He *never, ever* complained about those things. He was very, very funny and very insightful. He loved people and made friends with almost everyone.

But could I live with those explosions? The shrapnel of pointed words?

When Robert came home with his jacket thrown over his arm, his face was filled with concern. He couldn't miss the obvious signs that I'd been in utter torment. "What's wrong?"

"You … you … ," I tried to get through fresh tears. "You were out with somebody. You were out on a date."

He turned away, walking through the living room toward the bedroom. I didn't know if I should follow him or leave. At the door of the bedroom, he turned around, placing his hand on the doorjamb, leaning into it. "No, I wasn't out on a date. I was out with Rick."

Rick. Robert's friend.

"We just had dinner at a nice place, that's all."

I sank to the floor. "I can't do this anymore, Robert. I want to come home."

He didn't move. Didn't shout with delight. Didn't scold me. "Are you sure?"

"We can't be how we've been, though."

Robert looked at the floor. "I know. I've been awful."

I froze, unsure of what I was hearing. Did he finally see?

"It's going to be hard for me, though," Robert said. "I know I need to change. But I don't really know how."

"We'll have to give it one hundred percent," I said.

"I'm willing if you are," Robert said.

I nodded. "We'll give it our best shot."

"When will you move home?" he asked, looking at me with eyes filled with so much love and hope.

"Tomorrow."

I drove back to the apartment, wondering at what I had just done. Something inside had told me I needed to go home, and here I was obeying that nudge, not even knowing where it came from. I wasn't going home because I believed that Robert could change or that I sincerely wanted him back. I wanted to be with my kids. I wanted to be home. However, I would honor my promise of giving a hundred percent. I just wasn't sure that we could untangle this mess we'd made.

chapter 19

Wedding Rings

They say lightning doesn't strike the same place twice. They're wrong. The unexpected lightning bolt of stardom had hit our family — *twice* — and changed the whole dynamic of our marriage and family life.

We married with the knowledge that we'd never have money, that Robert's small salary would mean tight living if I was to stay home with the kids. Dad would be the powerful leader in finance, experience and wisdom. Mom would sit contentedly in the shadows, raising happy children to go to college and get married. When Hollywood struck, we weren't prepared for what it would do to us inside and out. We weren't prepared for our kids making more money than we did. Or for the abundance of travel I got to do, and the people I got to meet. We weren't prepared for how it would change the expectations we had for our marital roles or how it would radically change the dynamics of our traditional marriage.

Once we reconciled, it took a lot of hard work for us to see the places where we were behaving in damaging ways toward the other. Or where our initial presumptions about who we would be as marital partners had to be redefined. Everything had to be redefined.

I wish I could say it was easy from that moment of fragile reconciliation forward. It wasn't. Sometimes I still wondered if our marriage would work. But I had committed to one hundred percent and would continue to give one hundred percent.

Robert came to tape nights with Barb more often.

The thing that *did* change from that point forward was Robert. He watched his mouth, his tone, his word choice, and his actions. He didn't blow up anymore. His tenderness toward us took root and began to grow.

He came more often to tape nights. He suspected there had been another man in my heart, and discovered who it was. Yet, he still treated Steve respectfully and without malice.

I also wish I could say that my feelings for Steve immediately took flight. Unfortunately, I still looked at him with the same longing as before. I would turn away from it, but it was there, lingering. I had let my feelings for him get a hook-grip into my heart, and there they stayed.

I joined Robert and the girls in their now-regular attendance at church. At first I resented the fact that it took him so many years to go to church. It wasn't fair that *now* he decided to go. Why hadn't he gone before? Soon, I stopped grumbling and just accepted it as something good, and an answer to so many prayers.

I didn't always understand what the preacher taught, but I learned so much about living the Christian life. I still wanted to be good. I had failed miserably by my attempt at having an affair, but figured Jesus had died for *all* my sins, so I was okay.

Kirk started making choices on the set that differed from the old Kirk, evidence that there was something different about him. It became obvious to everyone—cast and crew alike. He saw himself as a role model for his hundreds of thousands of fans, and didn't want to fail them in that. He wanted Mike Seaver to be the same role model. So he asked the script writers to make sure that Mike Seaver did not do anything that would lead kids astray. In their frustration, the writers wanted Kirk to see that he was not Mike Seaver. Mike Seaver was initially mischievous and dove into things without thinking, but ultimately made the right decision. Kirk did not want Mike Seaver to party hard, sleep around, or do other things he knew would harm kids who wanted to emulate him. Tension on the set grew as Kirk's faith and commitment to Christ grew.

The girls also had new faith. The best day of my life was when most of us were baptized together (minus Robert and Melissa who were baptized later) and I recommitted my life to the Jesus I knew as a child. Now our family talked about faith. A little hesitantly at first, and more after it became the fabric of our lives. Robert didn't mind attending church anymore, but now said, "I'll give faith more thought after I retire."

Tiny Bridgette got a job as a stand-in for Candace on *Full House*. They needed someone about Candace's size so when the cameramen practiced adjusting angles and height, they would know where Candace would be during the actual filming. Bridgette loved her job and did very well at it. She even landed roles as a guest and an extra on the show, fulfilling her childhood dream of being able to perform one day.

Melissa graduated from high school, moved out, and, true to her father's dream, went to college. She decided to put herself through college on her own, waiting tables.

Kirk decided to "let me go" as his manager since he was old enough and wise enough in the business to make his own decisions. He also changed agents. He appreciated all that Iris had done for him throughout the years, but felt he needed to find an agent who better understood his faith and would work with him on appropriate roles.

Candace happily continued to work. Because she grew up on the set, *Full House* was like being with family all day, every day. Her dressing room was a part of the large sound stage, rather than a trailer. I decorated it with white wicker furniture to make it feel more homey and bright. Each season we hung new pictures or posters on the wall, keeping up with a teenager's changing tastes.

We continued our trips to Big Bear with friends, family, and Make-A-Wish or Starlight Foundation children. Hollywood swarmed around us, but no longer sucked us up. If Robert or I saw even a glimmer of arrogance in Kirk or Candace, we nipped it right there, reminding them of who they were and who they were not. I quietly bought some of the magazines that talked about the kids or our family and tucked them away for memory's sake. I didn't want to make a big deal out of them, because I knew that would puff up Candace and Kirk, and cause Melissa and Bridgette to feel small. I refused to do anything that would ostracize Melissa and Bridgette. They were great girls with fabulous personalities. I would dare anyone to treat them as lesser people simply because they didn't have television shows or movies on their résumés.

Parties, travel, laughing, having fun—those things didn't stop. The glamour of Hollywood continued, and we tried to remain the same, loving, tight-knit, "normal" family we had always been. Once away from the sets, life at home didn't change. All the kids still had a curfew, and we still encouraged their friends to come to our house, rather than the kids going to the homes of others. The girls were one another's best friends. They clung to each other like a clique—sharing, giggling, rolling their eyes about what I had done dumb this time.

People wondered why we stayed in our tract home. Robert had added on to it, so it was bigger than a cracker box, and he did a lovely job. There was plenty of room to have parties and gatherings. We'd been there for so long and had made it what we enjoyed. It held most of our family memories. Why move? It was *home*. We didn't need anything more than what we had.

We lost some of our friends along the way. It saddened us no end when people withdrew, quit calling, and stopped responding to our calls. One of our dear neighbors lit into Robert one day, "Get out!" he shouted. "Get out of the neighborhood! You don't belong here. We don't want you here."

Such things shocked us. We hadn't changed as far as we knew. Busier, sure. But we included our friends in any invitations we could. We invited friends to tape nights and to parties at our home as we always had.

Although we'll never truly know, some have suggested that it was probably jealousy. They want what you have and are angry they can't have it. They don't want to be around you to be reminded of all the dreams and desires they haven't achieved.

Not long after I moved back home, there was another filming trip to Hawaii. This time Robert went with us.

My relationship with Robert was still tentative and unsure. We were trying, but it felt like we were always doing some sort of sidestep around one painful issue or another. We didn't respond explosively as we used to, but things could still be awkward. I hoped this trip to Hawaii would shake something loose, as though some invisible ropes bound us to something we no longer wanted to be connected to.

As a surprise, Robert went to the swankiest restaurant on the island, The Swan Court—a restaurant with black and white swans swimming in a pond near the tables—to make a reservation. The Swan Court refused. "There is no way," he was told. "You must reserve months in advance."

Robert, feeling frantic, asked to see the manager. "You see, sir," he said, hating to grovel, but desperate to get a table. "I'm trying to get back with my wife. I've bought her a new set of wedding rings, and I'd like to give them to her in your restaurant tomorrow night."

The manager shook his head. "No, sorry. It's impossible."

Robert decided to play the card he hated. "I'm here with my son, shooting for television."

"Who is your son?" the manager asked.

"Kirk Cameron."

A visible change came over the manager. "Kirk Cameron is your son?"

"Yes, sir."

"Would you like to be here at six or eight?"

The following night to celebrate our eighteenth anniversary, Robert told me to dress up. He escorted me along the beach to this beautiful restaurant as though I were his queen. Our table was the best—overlooking the ocean. As the sun set in golden hues, melting into the ocean, we talked a lot, Robert's voice so gentle and sweet—full of a kindness I had missed.

At the end of the meal, the waiter brought a dessert plate and set it before me. On it was a black velvet box. I opened it. A beautiful set of wedding rings glinted. They were loaded with large diamonds—an extravagance we could not normally afford.

Robert took the rings and slid them on my finger. "These rings are a symbol of a new start in our life together." He looked into my eyes. "A new chapter. They also represent a new Robert. I love you, Barbara."

I looked at the rings and at the face of the man I knew I loved. The harshness had been erased by something I couldn't define. It didn't matter. I had hope.

chapter 20

Dreamer

I'm a dreamer. I admit it. I always think that if I achieve my biggest dream, I'll be satisfied and never want another thing again. Nope! I'm like a little girl in a store, begging her mommy for some toy or piece of candy. She promises, "If you buy me this, I'll *never* ask for anything *ever* again." Of course, the next time she goes to the store, something new will catch her eye.

Well, that's me. I dreamed my kids would get *one* commercial. That happened. And then I asked for another. And then I asked for a series or a television movie. I asked for Bridgette to have some acting roles.

I had seen all those dreams come true—all four of my children had been on television in one capacity or another. And my mind, like the little kid in the store, frantically searched for another big dream.

Since Kirk had turned eighteen and decided that he didn't need me to manage him anymore, I had a little more time. Managing only one child who was involved in a series didn't require nearly as much energy as when there were two involved in many auditions. Still, I wanted to continue working, and staying in the entertainment industry was my first choice. I knew this world, knew how to navigate it.

One dream kept nagging at me, and I kept putting it away—the one I'd had since I was in high school: to run my own business.

When I told Robert of my dream, he encouraged me. "Sure, Barb. Do whatever you want."

"What do you think I should do?"

He gave me that same grin I fell in love with at the beach so many years ago. "You can obviously do anything you try for, darlin'."

I considered my options. I could manage other actors—but I didn't really care for some of the hard-nosed cold-calling that job required. I'd have to be selling my client aggressively. Being a pleaser would make the type of aggression I needed a rather foolish and nearly impossible task. Besides, I believed child actors needed their parents, not outsiders, to be their managers.

Our attorney, Frank Stewart, suggested I open an agency—my closet dream for years.

"What? Me?" Although I'd dreamed about it, I really didn't think I had what it took to make that huge dream come true. "What do I know about running an agency?"

Frank looked at me, his eyes warm, yet serious. "A lot more than you think. You have many connections. You've worked closely with an agency for many years. You know a lot of parents with acting children, casting directors, producers. You'd be perfect for it."

Throughout the years I'd carefully observed agents, talked with moms about their agent stories, and heard horror stories, as well as glowing reports. I'd heard about the agents who treated the kids poorly, speaking to the family harshly and rudely. I'd had the great experience of working with Iris who protected her kids with a fierce loyalty and still took care to not keep nonworking kids on the roll too long.

I had considered what I'd do if I could be an agent, how I would treat kids and parents. I'd tell them the truth about the business. I'd shepherd them, and make sure no one took advantage of them. I would make this something that involved the family, rather than only the child. I would help parents remain parents, rather than letting the child take over as reigning family tyrant. I would assist the parents, helping them navigate these shark-infested waters of Hollywood so they could keep their children safe.

Sitting in the bleachers on the *Full House* set, I pondered the idea. Using Janice Sweetin, Jodie's mom, for a sounding board, I walked through my options. She listened and encouraged.

The more I thought about it, the more excited I got. Nervous, but excited. And I decided to go for it.

One day, as a friend and I drove through Woodland Hills, I pointed to the Warner Center Trillion Building. "That's where I want my agency office," I said. "Top floor."

"Really?" he said. "I just happen to know that there is an office available on the fifteenth floor. Do you want to see it?"

"Are you kidding? Yes!"

By the end of the next day, I had my office exactly where I'd dreamed it would be. I signed the lease, filed for my business license, registered with the Screen Actor's Guild, sent in my three letters of recommendation, and Barbara Cameron & Associates, A Talent Agency was in business!

Now here I was, on the Iris side of the desk, calling children to say lines for me, watching for that spark that says they have something going on inside. Watching for the kid who can take direction well. Interviewing the kids without their parents to be sure this was something *they* wanted to do. I had seen too many parents push children who weren't ready or interested in the business, and I didn't want to encourage that practice.

I loved the kids—as far as I was concerned, they were my children. I took great care of them and felt an absolute responsibility in getting them work, doing everything I could to get them on a series, doing commercials, or acting in a movie. When I got someone a part, I had a great feeling of accomplishment. I never had anyone receive an Academy Award, but my reward was in helping others and in knowing that I knew that I was the best agent I could be. It was a lot of hard work, with the roller-coaster ride of emotions, rejection, and successes—all the stuff that I had lived through with my own children.

Each morning, I woke very early to go through the breakdowns that arrived via fax all day and into the night. Each breakdown had lists of who was looking for actors for any type of commercial, television series or movies, or feature films. Then it broke down into specifics of the casting person, the project, commercial or production company, type of character, and the description of the character including age, sometimes height, weight, hair and eye color. I went through my files, finding the children who best fit the parts described. I pulled their headshots and résumés, tucked them into envelopes labeled with some identifying information for the casting director, and drove thirty minutes to Studio City. I took the packets to a drop-off point where a messenger service would pick them up and distribute them to the appropriate casting directors. These packets needed to be at the service before the 12:30 pick-up. After drop-off, my assistant and I would head to our favorite restaurant—The Good Earth—for lunch, then go back to the office and start over.

Throughout the day we interviewed new clients, read through the piles of mail requesting representation, and the best part of all— informed parents that their child had landed a part.

There was one aspect of my job that I dreaded—negotiations. I wanted to complete all negotiations in the first conversation because negotiation sessions were so uncomfortable. Yet, the offer from the studio almost never was appropriate for the part. After receiving the initial call, I took down all the information and said that I would get back to them. Then I'd come back with an offer, which they, of course, always thought was ridiculous. So then they would come back to me and give their unacceptable second offer. I'd go back to them and give another offer, and it went back and forth until we came to a place of agreement.

In the beginning, I felt I had no idea what I was doing. I spoke with other agents and friends who might know something about the business of negotiation and gleaned some helpful information from them. In time, I got better at it, learning after the fact that I had negotiated much better than the other agents. Yet I never felt truly comfortable in this role.

I did, however, enjoy the rest of the work. I discovered I had a good eye for children, a good eye for what Hollywood and casting directors were looking for. I saw in many of these actors a raw talent, knowing that all they needed was a bit of grooming and a chance to get in front of a casting director. I enjoyed watching their careers blossom as their dreams of acting and performing came true. Others worked hard at their craft, and were talented, but the opportunities for them were not there.

I took on clients who might not have been accepted by anyone else, knowing that they had a great character about them that might fit some of the quirkier parts of show business.

As many agents do, I took risks. I saw many successes that delighted me—such as Christine Lakin (Al on *Step By Step*). I found Christine during a trip to Atlanta, Georgia, when I attended a community theater group. Christine impressed me greatly, standing out from the rest. I searched out her mother after the performance and suggested that if she were ever in Hollywood, to please come and see me. Later that spring we got a call letting us know that the Lakins were coming to L.A. Christine had sent us an audition tape where she performed a monologue from *Irreconcilable Differences*. It was fabulous. When Christine came to L.A. I had the camera operators from *Full House* tape Christine's monologue on professional film. I sent the tape over to Miller-Boyett Productions. When Bob Boyett saw the tape, he called me and said that the girl was talented, but he didn't have anything for her at that time. A few months later he called back and said they were recasting for *Step By Step* and asked if Christine could come and audition. Christine and her mom flew to L.A. for the audition, after which Christine booked the job and never went home.

Other unknowns at that time came through my agency. Now they have become huge stars—such as Britney Spears and Hillary Duff. Kal Penn (Kumar in *Harold & Kumar Go To White Castle*), Jurnie Smollett and the entire Smollett family (*On Our Own*), Giuseppe Andrews (*Two Guys and a Girl*), Brian Hooks (*Eve*), Sylvester Terkay, Peter Navy Tuiasosopo, Mikala (singer), Michael Horton, Shailene Woodley, and Blake Bryan all have successful careers today.

I also represented Candace after she left Iris Burton's agency. I helped her land movies of the week and other jobs.

After a year at the Trillion Building, I decided to really take a huge step—one that I had been told continuously couldn't be done. I moved my business to our home. That section of the garage that used to house the fan club received another make-over and became the agency headquarters. I'd been told no one would go to the valley for interviews, and I proved them wrong. For the next 11 years, I ran a successful agency from those offices.

I also hired a man named Jonathan Koch, who became my business partner and friend. He'd entered our family circle in the usual way—as a friend of Kirk's, and who was then grilled by Robert to be sure his intentions were on the up and up.

Jono, as we called him, brought to the agency a remarkable sense of business that helped my agency grow. He was great at cold-calling,

Candace and Barb at a personal appearance.

something else that brought a paralyzing sense of awkwardness to me. He called everyone who needed to know we were in business.

He had the great idea that the first Christmas we really blitz the casting directors and production companies. I made dozens of my chocolate cookies, putting them in individual packages with ribbons around them. Candace and Melissa dressed like reindeer, Bridgette like an elf, and Jono as Santa Claus, and Robert carried around a boom box playing Christmas songs. This simple marketing stunt really helped launch the agency. People remembered when they looked at our clients' packets.

I started out slowly, but eventually I carried double the load of clients that Iris had. After time, I discovered that many was simply too unwieldy, and realized why Iris had kept her numbers trim. I found the most success through commercials, although I did place some actors in other types of work. A number of my children acted in pilots that didn't get picked up, and that was a bit disappointing for us all.

A lot of times with children's agencies, once you get an actor on a series or in a big movie, the bigger agencies come and entice the actor away from you. They will tell the parents everything they want to hear, promising that they would land bigger parts than I ever could. The truth was, no one could predict if or when any child would land a part. And I had access to all the same information as other agencies. Because I cared about each family that I took on, it hurt to see the family follow after empty promises. But as a parent who was in the same situation, I know what it's like to want to get the best for your child.

However, my work was steady and paid the bills, and I had a lot of *fun* doing it. For me, that was the biggest reason to stay in business.

While running the agency, Jono and I put our heads together to create a company called Gravy Train Productions. Jono was President and CEO. This company was a talent promotional agency. Our role was to take the kids in a television series, and promote them to the public. We arranged for appearances where the child signed autographs, creating a stronger fan base, and therefore, greater potential for more work. Having fans is critical to keeping your actor's name in front of the viewing audience, and their desire to see him or her brings more opportunities to the child.

Jono arranged the appearances, so he also helped me take Candace all around the country. We three had a blast hanging out together, doing fun things. These appearances could be quite stressful. In order to fly cheaply, we took red-eye flights. Not being a "morning person," Candace had a tough time waking and often felt cranky. But when in front of the crowds, she always put on her friendly face. Candace, more than most child actors, had a presence about her that made her fans feel she was real and approachable.

Once we went to New Brunswick, Canada, where we encountered a situation that we'd never seen before. A mall had asked Candace to come and had set up a table and a chair for Candace to sign photos and autographs. When we got near the mall, we saw an endless line of cars — three miles long, waiting to get into the mall! The limo had to drive on the berm to get close to the mall. Fans swarmed the car, running all through the stopped cars to get to the limo. Inside the mall, we found 25,000 fans! When Jono saw how disorganized the event was, and that mall administrators had not followed protocol, he feared for Candace's safety. As he considered, he realized that if we tried to leave immediately, there would be a bigger riot.

Kirk and Barb at a theme park in Georgia during a personal appearance.

So for the next four hours, Jono guided the line as Candace signed autographs without looking up. People chanted and threw money on the tiny stage where Candace perched in her chair. It was an insane madhouse ... and a bit frightening.

Overall, the appearances were enjoyable, and Jono tried to weave in fun things for us to do. Jono and Candace loved to ride roller-coasters, so if we were in a town with an amusement park, the two of them took a limo ride to the park, and were ushered right up to the rides they wanted to go on. Other times, Jono combined our trips with sporting events—which he and Candace also loved. We kept that business for six years.

The agencies gave me the freedom to take care of Candace when I needed to. As long as I rose early to read the breakdowns, got my packets of information together, and delivered them, I had the freedom to run errands in the middle of the day, or run to the *Full House* set and watch for a couple hours and gab with Janice and any other moms who might be there.

One day, while putting our heads together, Chelsea Noble appeared on the set for a guest appearance. "I would *love* for her to be my daughter-in-law," I confided to Janice.

"She is absolutely gorgeous," Janice said. She gave me a pointed look. "And dating John Stamos."

I shrugged. "That doesn't stop me from dreaming. She has the heart and soul of a girl I could see Kirk marrying. She'd be so good for him." I had seen Chelsea around the set a lot, watching how she handled situations and people. I saw her tenderness, her bright spirit, her sense of play, yet the ability to go very deep emotionally.

Janice sighed. "She is very sweet."

Not six months later, Chelsea and John broke up. Janice and I took the news with wide-eyed glee. "She's available!" Janice shrieked.

"Yeah!" I said, laughing. "But how in the world are we going to get her together with Kirk?"

We both laughed at our silly mother-dreams.

A few weeks later, I took a lunch break from the agency to corner Janice in the bleachers. "You'll never guess," I said, barely able to contain my delight.

"You booked a superstar."

"Better than that," I paused, looking around to be sure no one else was listening. "Chelsea has a guest role on *Growing Pains*."

"No!"

"Yes!"

"What if?"

"I KNOW! Can you believe it?"

Janice shook her head. "I wish I had the magic wand you do. Everything you touch comes out right."

I gave her a look and she sobered. "Well, almost everything," she clarified.

I couldn't wait for the taping of the show. What I didn't know is that Kirk was also very smitten with Chelsea. He kept it quiet, but he really, really wanted her on the show. When she landed the part of Kate after an audition, he couldn't have been more delighted.

On the third show where Kate appeared, Kirk freaked when he saw that a scene involved a kiss. He was really nervous about Chelsea because he was actually interested in her. He thought she was very beautiful. They'd talked a little, but he still hadn't let the cat out of the bag that he liked her.

One day she found Kirk outside his trailer, playing worship songs on his guitar. "Are you a Christian?" she asked.

"Yes, I am," Kirk said.

"I am too." She gave him that smile that totally won him over in a heartbeat.

All week during rehearsals, Kirk avoided the kiss by getting to that point in the script saying, "And then, Mike kisses Kate," and they'd complete the scene without a kiss.

On tape night, when the first kiss would be in front of the audience, Kirk couldn't stand the nerves that wracked his stomach. Resorting to standard operating procedure for both Kirk and Mike Seaver, he ran to the prop room, looking for something he could use. Digging through the first aid kit, he found some Anbesol, and knew it would be perfect. Anbesol, as most mothers know, is for numbing the gums of babies who have teething pain. Kirk spread some on his lips, and kissed Chelsea.

Five seconds later, Chelsea's lips went numb. She tried to get her lines out, but her lips didn't work properly. Her eyes went wide as she attempted again to say her lines.

Kirk flashed his signature smile at the camera and said coolly, "That's just the effect I have on women. My kisses are electrifying."

Chelsea had no idea what had happened to her, but once she realized Kirk pulled this crazy stunt, she thought it was so funny. Until then, she had no idea how fun Kirk could be. And he didn't disappoint—he continued to surprise her with funny, goofy things that made her laugh.

Once Chelsea's role as Kate officially ended, the studio wanted to keep her. They saw the growing chemistry between her and Kirk. Chemistry equals viewers; more viewers equal higher ratings; higher ratings equal more money. So Chelsea landed a permanent place until the show ended in 1991. As the romance between Mike Seaver and Kate blossomed, so did the romance between Kirk and Chelsea. In the summer of 1991, another of my dreams came true when they married on July 20 in Chelsea's hometown of Buffalo, New York.

All this time, Robert continued to woo me. Occasionally, I kept him at arm's length, still hurt and angry at how he'd treated me in the past, and afraid he might slip back. Sometimes I thought about Steve, foolishly wondering how life would be with him. And sometimes

Robert did slip up. But for the most part, he changed. The girls watched in wide-eyed wonder. "Is that really Dad?"

He took me out to a nice dinner one evening. With our appetizer came freshwater pearl earrings, with dinner, a necklace, and for dessert, a matching bracelet. "I love you, Barb," he said. "I'm sorry I haven't treated you better in the past. But I'm giving it my all now."

And boy, did he ever! He and my friend Shelene's husband, Brice, came up with "The Perfect Weekends." These weekends—sometimes just one day, sometimes overnight—took Shelene and me on surprise trips—local and distant—for romance, fun, and connecting. One of the most memorable started with a personal ad in the newspaper that gave hints to our next location (Victoria's Secret, where we each received a wrapped gift and a map). We ended up in San Diego with a dozen roses each in crystal vases, personal massages by our husbands, then a dinner cruise on the bay.

One day my sister Joanne brought over a baby a friend of hers cared for as a foster parent. I took one look at this helpless, motherless child, and fell in love. Her name was Joyce, and I began to baby-sit her frequently. I took her to the set of *Full House* where the entire cast would come and coo over her when they weren't in a scene. She was an incredibly loved and cared for baby.

One by one, my children had left home to do one thing or another. Even the ones who lived at home were driving and in charge of their own lives. It was too early for grandchildren, and I missed having babies.

In time, feeling the void in my life as the "empty nest" syndrome was upon us, I decided I wanted to foster babies as well. Robert again supported me, although I have a feeling he thought I was a little crazy. I decided to take only babies on a short-term basis, caring for them until the system found a good home for these little ones. This seemed to be the best way to go since they were "portable," and I could just pack them up and take them everywhere with me. They had their own space in the office, and they had more love poured out on them in the short months or year they were with me.

I prayed for these precious children as I cared for them, wanting them to find homes with loving parents. I knew I was only temporary, but if I could lavish them with love as they waited for a permanent

One of our foster children, Tatianna, became our godchild.

home, I felt they would have a solid foundation to grow from. As far as I was concerned, these children were no burden. They became a part of our family until we tearfully said good-bye. However, there was more joy than sorrow. Two of them went to loving homes, and one went to a relative of hers, and we never had contact with her again. I have received pictures as they have grown, and those framed photos join the legions of family photos around my home. One of our foster children, Tatianna, became our godchild. She is now nine years old and lives with her mother and brother, and we see her throughout the year.

It saddened me when I realized that perhaps it was time to move on, and leave that part of life behind. My own grandchildren were beginning to arrive, and I wanted to make sure I had enough time and energy for them. I didn't regret a moment of being a foster parent, but I, more than anyone, knew that a woman needs to flow with the seasons life brings. And it was time for me to walk boldly forward into the next season and enjoy the unique blessings it would offer.

chapter 21

Callaway Gardens

Dark-eyed Melissa Centrella seemed like a normal, happy, active child until she turned seven. That June, wearing a green and black dance outfit, her thick, black hair falling below her waist, she danced her heart out in a recital. By December, she couldn't get out of a wheelchair.

The doctors diagnosed her as having a progressive, painful, neurological disorder called dystonia—a disease that causes twisting and spasms of the limbs. The muscles pull into themselves, doing the opposite of what they should. They contract when they are supposed to relax, and relax when they are supposed to contract. The result is that the patient cannot control what her body does—she is at the mercy of her twisting limbs.

Melissa, an only child, had parents who devoted their lives to try to give her the best life possible. They contacted the Starlight Foundation, which called to ask her if she had three wishes. She did.

Melissa, in love with Kirk, never missed an episode of *Growing Pains*. She was also a fan of *Full House*. Speaking with much difficulty due to the disease, she said, "My first wish is to meet Kirk Cameron, my second wish is to meet Candace Cameron, and my third wish is to get better … in that sequence."

Opposite page: *Pizza for the gang at Camp Callaway*

In January 1990, the second of her dreams came true as she spent a day on the set of *Full House*. The next day she would have her first dream come true in a visit to a taping of *Growing Pains*. I met Melissa and her mother as they were leaving the set of *Full House*. Melissa grinned with a beautiful smile that lit her eyes. She had so much life trapped in her tiny, bent body. I squatted to talk to her, sharing with her that during the next night's show, she would get to see Kirk go out on a date with Chelsea. "I'll send a package of goodies for you with Kirk tomorrow. Would that be all right?"

Melissa said, "Thank you," in a weak voice, but everything about her shone.

At the taping of *Growing Pains*, Melissa was in heaven. After the show, Kirk gave her a dozen roses and the package I'd prepared with items from the shows. She mustered up all her energy to tell Kirk, "I love you."

The following year Melissa came back to Los Angeles to see the shows again, this time for her fourteenth birthday. Both shows threw birthday parties for her with cakes. I invited the family to our house for dinner where I gave Melissa a party as well.

Our whole family adored Melissa. She exuded a peace and joy even through her painful spasms. Because of Melissa and many other incredible, special children, we first began Camp Callaway, which later transformed into Camp Firefly.

Over the years of having children like Melissa come to *Growing Pains* and *Full House* with the Make-A-Wish and Starlight Foundations increased our love and concern for them. We made their visits as exciting as possible within the limits of what the studio would allow. I would take a vested interest in the families to make sure that their experiences were memorable ones. Yet we felt that having ill children come to a taping and sit for hours to receive only a picture and autograph was something—but not enough.

"Mom," Kirk said to me one day. "I think that, instead of looking for a film for me to do during hiatus, I'd rather do something for some of these sick kids."

"Like what?" I said, eager to do *anything* we could for them.

"Why don't we take them camping?"

I probably just stared at him, picturing a juggling act of getting oxygen tanks and wheelchairs over narrow, tree-lined trails. What about getting these seriously ill kids in and out of pit toilets?

"We had so much fun camping when we were kids," Kirk continued, excitement popping his words out even faster than normal. "Everyone should get a chance to be outdoors. What do you say, Mom? You think we could do it?"

"It sounds great. I'll look into it," I said, not wanting to crush his great dream, but also having no idea how we could make that happen.

I talked to God about it, telling Him that if there was any way He could help it to happen, I'd be very grateful.

I shared the idea with our friend and entertainment attorney, Frank Stewart—the same man who encouraged me to start my agency. Frank told me about a place called Callaway Gardens near Atlanta, Georgia, where he spent his childhood vacations. He said it was a perfect place to hold a camp for these children. He suggested that I take a trip down there and check it out.

The moment I saw the grounds of the Gardens I knew I'd found where we could hold "camp." Callaway Gardens has 13,000 acres of gardens, golf course, protected lands and waters—including a sandy beach on one side of a lake. The abundance of flowers was incredible: azaleas and many other gorgeous flowers blooming all throughout the property. They have horticultural and butterfly centers, nature shows, and miles of trails. For activities they provided fishing, paddleboats, water-skiing, jet skiing, water-boarding, bicycle trails, hayrides, a participation circus, and a boat for a sunset dinner cruise. For lodging the families, we could take advantage of Callaway's villas.

It was amazing and perfect!

Thoughts, plans, and ideas rushed into my head. How could we do this? How could we make this happen? To cover everything for these families would get very expensive.

I called Kirk, anxious to tell him all I'd seen. "Kirk! This is it! But it's going to take some money to do this."

"Mom, money doesn't matter. Helping these kids and their families is all that matters."

"Are you sure?"

"The sky's the limit, Mom. I trust you. You have great ideas. Go for it. Just make it special for these kids. I'll fund it all."

I hung up the phone, amazed at my teenage son's generosity.

Immediately, I started jotting down ideas and dreams. My associate, Lisa West, was very helpful in getting companies to donate services for some of the needs that we had. American Airlines helped us with the flights. Callaway allowed us to use their villas at a discounted rate. Mattel donated age-appropriate toys for all the children and their siblings. We filled welcome baskets with Barbie dolls, cars, trucks, and special toys for each family, which would be waiting in their villa when they arrived. We also had baskets filled with special items for the parents such as perfume, aftershave, nail polish, and new toiletries.

Nike supplied new shoes for everyone in the family. Side Out clothing sent scads of clothes, which we piled on the beds of the villas. Pepsi sent so many sodas, we filled the closet—floor to ceiling—in our villa with the extras to hand out during the week. We had more than enough of everything!

We selected six families to come to camp for a week's vacation. This included the whole family—mom, dad, and siblings. Many of our families didn't have the money to do something like this, and so We wanted this to be an event where they didn't have to worry about anything! From the time they left their homes to the time they got back, we provided everything for them. A limousine service picked them up at their homes to take them to the airport. In Atlanta, volunteers from the wish organization met them at the airport and took them to a private bus, which held an abundance of food, drinks, and fun games to pass the hour's drive to the Gardens.

We greeted the families at the gardens as they came off the bus. My heart filled with such joy to see each family and know that we had an entire week to share with them.

Squeals of delight, mixed with awed faces came over them as each family was presented with a Lexus luxury car for their use during the week, on loan from the local Lexus dealership.

Each family oohed and aahed over their car, piled in and took off toward their designated two- or three-bedroom villa, depending on the need. The elegant villas were nestled in the lush, beautiful, woodsy grounds, with the abundance of blooming azaleas lending a pink glow to everything.

We had decided that it would be fun to all eat together, and so we designated one area, which was close to everyone. The first evening, cautious families appeared at poolside for a barbecue, unsure what this week entailed, and what was expected of them. I suppose they were also a bit overwhelmed by what they'd already experienced.

Kirk, seeing that things were a bit stiff, took Bridgette aside. "Look, Bridge. I'm going to throw you into the pool with all your clothes on. I want you to fight and scream, but then let me."

Kirk's sisters are usually up for his games, so she went along with it. She went back to her seat and picked up her dinner plate. Minutes later, Kirk came up to her, and grabbed her. Bridgette fought and screamed, but eventually landed in the pool. She climbed out, grabbed a counselor, and in she went, too. That broke the ice, and soon many folks were soaked to the skin, laughing and teasing one another. Another time someone ended up with a bucket of ice dumped over him. Ice fights ensued to the delight of everyone.

In the morning, we served breakfast of scrambled eggs, hash brown potatoes, fruit, yogurt, cereal, coffee, tea, milk, juice, and assorted donuts catered around the pool area. We quickly learned that the appetites of these sick children were very small, so we adjusted the quantity so as not to waste too much food.

After breakfast each day, one ill child got to spend an hour alone with Kirk, doing whatever it was he or she wanted to do. Each child had the choice of fishing, boating, or just sitting underneath a shade tree and talking—any activity for that hour.

During the week, we also had many activities for the entire family to participate in if they wanted to.

Callaway hires Florida State University students as summer employees to run a variety of activities. We prearranged some of our activities through these students, such as water-skiing lessons. Some of these students ran a circus, which performed a couple times during the week. As a special treat for our children (especially the healthy siblings), the students helped them use whatever apparatus they wanted—even flying from the high trapeze bar. Accommodations were made so the sick children could do whatever they were capable of.

Some of our children were weak and tired easily, yet after a few days of fun-filled excitement, the focus on their illness seemed to disappear. The wigs of cancer patients came off. The prosthetics stayed in the villas. Well, most of the prosthetics.

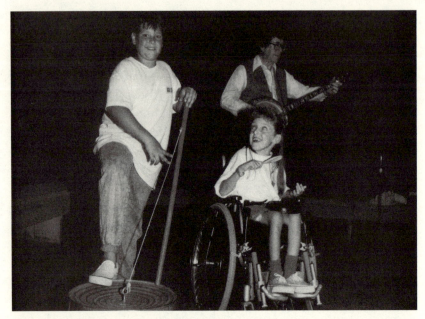

Kids putting on a show at Camp Callaway.

One of our girls, Bethany Anglin, had her arm amputated just below the elbow to stop her bone cancer. The surgery left a little knob of an elbow that she could move. She named her nub "Susie," and Susie would have conversations with people. Bethany's prosthetic arm, decorated with rings and bracelets, had a name as well—"Macy." Bethany showed the other kids how Macy worked, to the delight of them all. Soon Macy made the rounds, pinching people, grabbing things from them, and performing all sorts of mischief at the hands of whoever had gotten a hold of her this time.

Susie had a great personality, as did Bethany. We discovered Bethany threw a "birthday" party for Susie every February 2, the day Susie was "born." Bethany used Susie to talk to other kids about what happened to her arm. "This is Susie," she'd tell them. "Susie got really, really sick. The doctors tried to give her medicine, but she didn't get better." And sometimes she'd even put faces on Susie. And when Susie talked, she had a high-pitched voice.

Bethany, at nine, never complained, was never upset, knew a lot about a lot of things, was charismatic and fun to be around. She did everything camp had to offer. She water-skied, water-boarded, jet skied, walked the tightrope, and tried out the flying trapeze. She had such an amazing go-for-it attitude, that the Callaway Gardens ski team incorporated Bethany into their weekly show.

She and a boy her age, Austin, developed crushes on each other. So, one day, while a bunch of the kids were bike riding (the sick kids rode on the bike trail in golf carts driven by an adult), they discovered a tiny chapel in the woods. Stained glass windows let the sunlight spill buckets of colors onto the stone floor. Kirk got up the great idea that they should marry, so all the kids gathered in the chapel. Melissa and Bridgette fashioned a little flower crown for Bethany. When Kirk, the faux preacher said, "If there's anyone here who objects to this wedding, speak now, or forever hold your peace," Austin's little sister jumped up and shouted in her southern drawl, "Oh, no, you're not gonna marry my brother."

The dynamics of the week brought kids together in ways we couldn't have expected. Melissa and Bridgette understood the siblings of the sick kids. Attention in the real world naturally gravitated to the famous children, or the sick ones, while the siblings remained in the shadows.

The parents watched as miracles happened before their eyes. Their children didn't need the oxygen as much as they usually did. Their children had never eaten so well. They were fearless, trying everything they possibly could.

One evening, my children, with permission, disconnected some of the devices from a wheelchair-bound girl and lifted her into the hot tub. They supported her while she played to the extent that her body would let her. Her mom sat by, watching, tears streaming down her face. "She's never been in a pool," she said softly.

We drove the families around the zoo in a zebra-striped bus. One night we had a hayride to the farm barn where we had a barbecue. We ate barbecued chicken, barbecued ribs, corn on the cob, baked beans, soda, and even peach cobbler, while seated at tables decorated with red and white tablecloths. The group clapped and cheered the cloggers we'd hired to entertain.

The focus was not all on the sick children—or even the siblings. We knew that the parents often found their own needs lost in the overwhelming needs of their children. They'd sacrificed so much to care for their families. So we wanted to take care of the parents as well.

Moms appreciated the Mom make-over day, where they received the pampering they never had time for. I drove them to the local beauty salon for manicures, pedicures, and a new hairstyle. Some asked for a major make-over with drastic hair color changes or haircuts. They returned to their families feeling relaxed and beautiful!

While the moms got pampered, Robert took the dads golfing. The gardens have a beautiful golf course on the property. They had great conversations, laughing, male bonding—all the wonderful things that men enjoy and these dads didn't have the time or funds to do.

While all of this was going on, the kids were being entertained by Kirk, Chelsea, his sisters, and the counselors we had brought with us. The children made thank-you baskets for their moms and dads for all that they do. We presented the baskets to them that evening at a romantic restaurant—parents only. These moms and dads didn't have time for many—if any—romantic dinners, so we brought this special evening to them. They shared with each other heartfelt issues that only these parents can understand—about their struggles and joys. It was a time for each couple to rekindle intimate feelings for each other that may have been lost through their struggles.

While the parents were out to dinner with Robert and me, Kirk was back at Garden Central, having a pizza party with the kids, and singing songs accompanied by his guitar.

After the dinner, the parents picked up their children and took them home to bed. The next morning started the same way as the others had; with gathering by the pool for breakfast and then fishing, bicycle riding along the woodsy path, or just chilling out at the pool.

Just as laughter filled our camp days, the farewell day filled with tears. We knew that many of these children would not live until the next year's camp reunion. And many of those who did, still had fewer years ahead of them than most children. No one wanted to leave this place where they'd found acceptance, fun, and laughter, and made lifelong connections. Many tears of joy and sadness were shed during those good-byes.

The families boarded the bus back to the airport. Back in their hometowns, limousines met them at the airport to take them home. After camp, we sent each family a photo album of camp memories, photos taken by a photographer we'd hired for that purpose.

Chelsea and Kirk with Jillian Yee, one of our camp children, at Camp Callaway.

It was a week to remember for these children and their families—and us! The first week was so successful, we couldn't let that be the only one ever. And so, Camp Callaway continued. Melissa Centrella came, and we bonded even more deeply with her parents and her. She got sick during camp and had to be rushed to the hospital. Although her parents felt bad and wanted to go home, we encouraged them to come back to camp—which they did, completing a great week for all of them. We had kids like Callie who had cystic fibrosis. Even though she was dying right in front of us, she had an amazing spirit. A skinny girl—no more than skin and bones—she had a personality a hundred times bigger. Her contagious laugh and continual jokes kept us all laughing and enjoying being around her. And there was Mandy, who had lost a leg to cancer—and almost lost it again to Kirk who kept absconding with the prosthetic.

In the beginning, we chose the families from those who had visited the television shows. Today, families are chosen with the help of children's hospitals, doctors, and social workers throughout America. The families never know if they are being considered, and no applications from families are ever accepted. Kirk and Chelsea pray over each potential camp member, choosing them from piles of suggestions.

When Kirk and Chelsea married, they took over all the details for planning and running the camp, including putting aside a day before the camps each year to invite families from previous years to come to the Gardens for a reunion. As of 2006, the camp has been in existence for seventeen years, but has been renamed Camp Firefly. The camp is funded through fund-raising events and through the support of generous people who believe in the camp.

The relationships that I developed during those years are ones that I will always hold dear to my heart. I still have contact with families from these camps today and see some of the wish children, too. My own children still hang out with Bethany Anglin and her husband. Bethany's cancer was the type that needed to be in remission for thirteen years before she could be considered cured. She has recently celebrated that thirteen-year mark, and we couldn't be happier.

There were children who lived on for many years, some who are in remission, some who didn't even make it to their camp date because they had passed on. Melissa Centrella is our sweetheart to whom we had to say good-bye in 2005. Her parents were told she would not live to see thirteen, yet she lived to be twenty-five—twelve years of added joy for all of us. What a blessing these people are and have given my family and me so much joy in knowing them.

Barb and Robert with Melissa Centrella on her 21st birthday.

chapter 22

Paths of Glory

Looking back over my life, I couldn't believe all I had done and accomplished. This simple girl, lacking in self-confidence and believing she would live in shadows all her life, raised four kids to be wonderful human beings who were not only happy, but had come through relatively unscarred by an industry known to destroy children who dare enter its gates. Even my girls who didn't become famous actors did not get involved in drugs and made it safely through to adulthood. They could have become devastated and jealous over the fame and fortune their siblings received — but they didn't. I somehow managed to get my acting kids through the murky, dangerous waters of growing up on television series. I spoke to heads of large production companies and stood my ground on behalf of my children and the children of others I represented. I demanded what was best for them, but did it in a way that was respectful of the position of the person with whom I negotiated. I traveled all over the country and in various parts of the world with my children. I rode in limousines and private jets as a person of privilege.

I had the privilege of helping hundreds of dying children and their families to feel special for a reason other than being sick. I didn't know anything about these diseases, but learned and tried to accommodate their needs accordingly. I helped my son begin a "camp" where families could think about something other than the illness of their children for a week and where the siblings and parents of the sick ones could be in the limelight and pampered.

I gave out thousands of hugs and famous chocolate chip cookies. I ventured into two difficult businesses in the entertainment industry, flying in the face of what I was told could not be done, and ran another business managing my children's careers for ten years, fighting the battles unique to it, and winning ... most of the time. I negotiated well for my clients. Through the foster care program, I took in children who had no mothers to care for them, and loved them until they found parents to take them under their wings.

I had met people of power, and people of fame. I shook their hands, and ate meals with them. I appeared on television shows and in magazines.

In the eyes of most who knew me, by the standards of nearly anyone on earth, I had done well. My good deeds to those around me far exceeded the bad choices and shameful things I'd done. I told the truth far more than the very infrequent lie. I had remained physically faithful to my husband and my marriage. I never asked for my children to become famous, only that they have fun doing a commercial or a show. I didn't join the Hollywood expectations to grasp and claw for more "stuff" to own and flaunt money, but was very happy and content with what I had.

And yet, something as small as a fluttering feather told me that all was not right. I was missing something. But it was something I couldn't put my finger on.

Kirk encountered a man named Ray Comfort—an author who believed that the Church had gotten off-base in how they talked to people about what it took to become a Christian. It concerned him that huge numbers of people who decided to become Christians quickly lost faith and walked away. He discovered that instead of presenting the gospel as Jesus did, most modern preachers presented the message as making life happier and easier.

"Just try Jesus."

Or, "If you have Jesus, your life will be happy."

"Are you missing peace in your life? Try Jesus."

Kirk listened to this man's message, and it resonated with him. Kirk encouraged me to listen to Ray's message as well. He seemed so excited, bubbling over with new energy and passion. I could see in

Kirk's entire body that, unlike the moment when he first stood in front of Iris, hands in pockets, shoulders hunched a little, afraid, not knowing what was expected, he now knew what he needed to do. He knew what the director's instructions were, and how to deliver.

I tucked the CD titled "Hell's Best Kept Secret"* into our player, and messed around with all the remotes until I figured out which one worked and how to adjust the volume. I sat in my living room and listened. And listened again. And again.

What I heard struck the very core of my being. It answered questions that I had for almost forty years. It awakened something in me, something spiritual, that I had never experienced before. I had "believed in Jesus" since I was a little girl, but that faith never seemed to grow up. It never seemed to mature beyond my eight-year-old understanding. And a few questions had nagged at me over the years, keeping me from really embracing the Bible. Like, why would a loving God send anyone to Hell? After all, most people I knew were basically good people, just like I was. And why was it so critical that people believe in Jesus as opposed to another religious leader? Isn't the important thing that we live good lives and believe in God?

What I heard stripped away every false belief I'd had about God. I hadn't known they were false. Some beliefs had been close to the truth, but didn't quite finish it. It was as though someone told me how to bake a cake, but forgot to tell me to add flour. I had all the sweet things of God and His grace and His love well drilled into me. But I had missed something so profound that I ended up flat out on the floor of my living room, crying out to God.

Through Ray's passionate message about God's Moral Law, the Ten Commandments, I finally understood.

I suddenly realized something that shocked me. In retrospect, it was the most devastating and yet the most important truth I ever discovered. It totally changed the way I saw myself. It changed the way I saw what I had done to Robert, my children, and Steve. It especially changed my perception of my standing before God. It was as though I had lived my whole life in a dark room, and now I was standing in bright light.

---

* This message can be heard freely online at www.livingwaters.com/learn/
hellsbestkeptsecret.htm

I thought that I was basically a good person. God's Commandments showed me that I wasn't. I later heard a story that helped me to understand what happened that day. A little girl was watching sheep eat green grass. She thought how nice and white the sheep looked against the grass. Then it began to snow, and she thought how dirty those sheep now looked against the pure white snow. They were the same sheep, but they stood against a different background.

I was certainly good and pure compared to most people in Hollywood. But the day I understood the Commandments and what they required, it snowed. It snowed a storm. It was pure white driven snow, and with that purity as a background, I suddenly saw myself in truth.

The Ninth Commandment thundered, "You shall not bear false witness." I had lied ... not often, but I had lied to my husband, to my children, and to my friends. Deep down, I knew this made me, as horrible as it felt, a liar in God's eyes.

"You shall not commit adultery." I'd been an adulterer. No, I hadn't slept with Steve, but I'd sure considered it. In fact, I planned it all out. And Jesus taught in the Bible that if I even looked at a man desiring to be with him in a way reserved only for my husband, then I had committed adultery already in my heart.

"You shall not take the name of the Lord your God in vain." I'd used God's name in vain. Not often. But there were times when I was so angry, I said His name as a cuss word. When I'd done that, I'd disrespected God to the core of His being. I trashed Him and His holiness every time I'd spoken His name that way. I was a blasphemer.

I heard that God, as my Creator, commanded that He be first in my life. I thought He was. But that day I realized that I had created a god that worked for me. Just as Robert hadn't seen me in the past, and didn't take the time to really know me and who I was, I hadn't taken the time to ask God who He was and what He required of me. In my mind I created a god who fitted comfortably into my agenda, into what I wanted Him to be and do. I treated Him as my divine butler—a god that I called on when I wanted something. I was guilty of something that the Bible called "idolatry." I had violated the First and the Second of the Ten Commandments by making a god in my own image . . . and he was a god who didn't exist.

The true God had blessed me beyond my wildest dreams, and I had not only ignored Him, but I had repeatedly done things that were affronts to Him. I had pursued an affair, blamed Robert for my actions, hurt my children, and set a terrible example for those around me, all while justifying myself and calling myself a Christian. The thought that I had in any way offended God hadn't crossed my mind for a moment, but it began to make sense to me when I understood the serious nature of my sin. My big mistake was in thinking that God's standards were the same as mine. I had no idea that He considered lust to be adultery and hatred to be murder. I didn't know that He was perfect, and I didn't stop to consider that He saw and judged my thought-life.

On the CD, Ray gave an example of a "good" judge that really brought things into focus. A good judge can't let a devious criminal go. If the judge is good, he must see that justice is done. The criminal may say, "Judge, I did rape and murder that woman, but I want to let you know that I'm basically a good person, and I regularly do good things." The judge can't let a guilty criminal go. He must punish him. In fact, if the judge is good, he will be greatly angered by the man's terrible crime.

In God's eyes, I was like a devious criminal. A liar. An adulterer. A blasphemer. An idolater. I had a multitude of sins, and if God was good, I knew He must see to it that justice is done.

I didn't want to go through the rest of the Commandments. I dared not … commandments against stealing, dishonoring my parents, and ingratitude. I knew that I'd probably broken every single one of them, and in the process, angered God even further.

All my life I thought that I had loved Him. I said I wanted to be faithful to Him. In reality, I had seen Him as my security blanket. I went to God if I needed help in some selfish way.

If God judged me by His Commandments (His standard of goodness), I knew that I was deserving of Hell. My previous thought was that if God was "loving," He would never create such a place. Or at least, He would send only really bad people there—people like Hitler and mass murderers. But that's because I didn't understand how holy God is. I thought for a moment, should God look the other way when a man cuts the throat of an innocent person? Does He care about every right and wrong? Of course He does. Hell is God's "prison" for murders. But it's not just for murderers. Is He good enough to punish rapists? Of course He is. What about thieves, adulterers, liars, blasphemers, and idolaters? The Bible says so. That left me in big trouble. Judgment Day suddenly became a fearful reality to me.

I grieved. I sobbed. I called out to God. Before I had understood these things, I didn't think I needed to be "saved." Now I understood what the Bible meant about each of us having a heart that is "deceitfully wicked," and I desperately wanted God to take away the frightening consequences of my shameful behavior.

The gospel was something I'd known all my life, but suddenly it truly became "Good News." John 3:16 now made sense: "For God so loved the world that He gave His only begotten Son, that whoever believes in Him should not perish but have everlasting life." I had violated God's Law. I stood like a guilty criminal before Him. I had no defense. But the Bible says God is rich in mercy and made a way for me to be forgiven. He became a man, Jesus Christ, and suffered and died on the cross, taking my punishment upon Himself. Then Jesus rose from the grave and defeated death. God could now forgive me and give me everlasting life. He could dismiss my case, and allow me to live. What incredible love! All I had to do was turn from my sins once and for all, and trust in Jesus Christ to save me. If I would do that, the Bible says that God would make me righteous in His sight. He would wash me clean of my sin and "justify" me—not only forgive me, but actually forget about my sins as though I had never sinned in the first place. He would make me as white as snow. I finally saw how deep and wide God's love was for me, and my heart was ready to burst with gratitude!

I prayed through every wrong thing I could remember and for the ones that I could not, asking that He would reveal them to me. I didn't throw out a casual, "Oh, by the way, I'm sorry." Instead, truly asking for forgiveness came, as it must, from the devastated place inside that knew that without it, I couldn't go on. And before I could be forgiven, I had to be willing to move everything out of my heart that didn't belong there, then to seek God with all my heart.

I prayed that God would refresh me and that He would make me a new person.

My very private humbling of myself on the floor before God transformed my entire life. I had found the missing puzzle piece to my faith. I was no longer praying for God to change other people's hearts to suit my desires, but for God to change my heart to suit His. I didn't care anymore about what others thought of me. I only cared about whether or not my life pleased God. I found out what He wanted me to do by reading the Bible, and I made a habit of reading it every day. My personal agenda began to take a back seat.

I wanted now to work for Him—no matter what it was He asked. And it wasn't a burden. It became such a joy and my heart's exploding desire. I learned that joy and happiness aren't the same thing. And I decided I liked joy better because it lasted through the tearful, fearful times when happiness didn't. I had joy in knowing that no matter what horrible things life could bring me, God would see me through. He once and for all demonstrated His love for me on the cross, and I knew I no longer needed to fear anything—not even death.

Jesus said, "You shall know the truth and the truth shall set you free." I had no idea that my life's greatest adventure hadn't ended, but was ready to burst into something more wonderful than I could have ever dreamed.

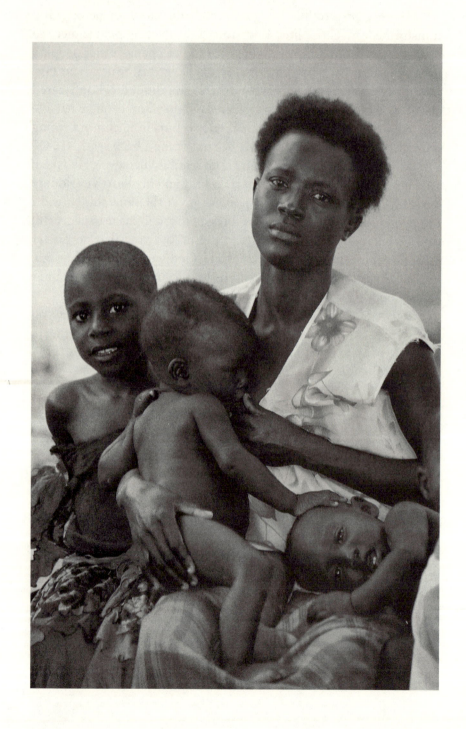

chapter 23

Africa

Hollywood seemed so far away. Rain came down in sheets, pouring from thatched roofs in thick waterfalls. For a moment, the tropical birds had stopped their rich trills and calls. The thick heat grew heavier. I had watched the storm move in, and waited until it passed over.

Africa.

No thrill of Hollywood, no excitement of meeting stars, no party, no beautiful clothing could even come close to fulfilling my heart as my job now. I had come to feed the children. I had come to feed the families.

As we stepped out of the 18-foot canopy-covered boat, children dressed in clothes left behind by missionary visitors and shipped from caring people around the world clustered around the dock to sing. Their voices rang pure and true.

In Africa we love the Lord.
In Uganda we love the King.
May all of Africa get His holiness,
May all of Africa get His holiness,
Uganda my homeland,
Uganda my homeland,
The pearl of Africa.

I opened my heart, letting these beautiful children inside. Their smiles lit up the already sun-bright morning. I wanted to take them all into a giant hug. Instead, we followed them to their village where mud huts, the size of walk-in closets, were clustered together. Mud and sticks—the kind the wolf could blow down with a huff and a puff.

A thick scent assaulted my senses. Something so dark and nasty, my brain could not sort it out. Rotting, burning garbage? Stagnant water? Unwashed bodies? Raw sewage? Could it be coming from the lake? Infested with parasites, leeches, and excrement from animal and human alike, it was putrid. And yet, it is the only water they have to use to wash their clothes. Later, I would get used to the smell, but it took days to adjust.

As often as not, a preteen girl would pull aside the worn and hole-pocked sheet used as a door to her hut, and invite a guest in. Within this tiny hut, banana leaf mats were rolled and set to one side. Children younger than she played on the dirt floor that held in the dank dampness. But the girl would smile, her grin taking over her face. "Welcome to my home."

"Your home?"

"Yes."

It wasn't long before the sad reality overcame me—the young girl was the "mother" of these six little ones.

So I sat on the floor to join them, finding a bottle of bubbles in my small pack. The bit of light from the front door illuminated rainbows in the bubbles. The children were in awe. They watched only for a moment, and then they were on their feet, chasing the bubbles, trying to catch them, giggling when they exploded in a soundless, moist *pop*!

More children arrived, and we moved to a larger place where all could see and play. They sang me a song. I sang one for them and taught it to them. We played Rock, Paper, Scissors. I told them about the Ten Commandments. I passed around sticks of gum, and soon they all looked like little sheep chewing intently. I took pictures of them with my digital camera, then showed them their faces on the screen. Most had never seen themselves before, and couldn't contain their awe.

Some children kicked around a "soccer" ball made of scrunched plastic grocery bags wrapped with strips of banana leaves until it resembled a ball.

Soon the children left to catch a chicken for dinner, adding it to the frightening-looking things resting in their small pot ready to be set on the rock over a very small fire. For water, they balanced a yellow container on their heads—containers that, when filled, weigh more than they do.

We had brought food for this village. Rice and beans, which we scooped out with small bowls into whatever container they may bring. In long lines they waited patiently, some with blue plastic washtubs balanced on their heads. Adorned in clothing with colors of the rainbow. Dusty feet. Some of the children with the bloated bellies of malnutrition—a sign that death was around the corner. Small flies clustering around their eyes, noses, and lips, no longer batted away. Beautiful children, some with dark chocolate eyes so bright, their faces elicited smiles in the pale faces of the *munguzoo* (white person).

I marveled that the images I had seen as hazy dreams decades before were now real images and people before me.

The journey to Africa began as a result of that day on the carpet in my living room. I slowly closed down the agency. It was tough to say good-bye to the kids, but not to the games needed to play in negotiations. It wasn't hard to say good-bye to the foulmouthed execs around whom I felt belittled and small. Nor to the cold-calling and game-playing.

I began to work for The Way of the Master, Kirk's and Ray Comfort's new ministry, answering e-mail questions and comments from the many viewers of their television show of the same name. The e-mails are full of confusion, heartache, and sometimes anger. I research to answer the question, then reply the best I can, sometimes sending out materials to more clearly answer the questioners. The intellectual stimulation is fascinating and challenging. To help others break through the confusion to the eye-popping, "I get it!" is much more satisfying than finding a kid a job on a television series.

During the 2002 Christmas season, a speaker came to our church, telling us about the Children's Hunger Fund (CHF), a nonprofit, nondenominational Christian organization, which helps hurting and

hungry children and their families all across the United States and developing countries.

My heart went out to the children we had seen through the presentation, and I wanted to do something tangible to help. So Robert and I took seven boxes (one for each of our grandchildren) to fill with food for the Family Pak Program.

At Costco we filled our cart with the suggested items, such as canned goods, toiletries, rice, beans, dry milk, and some goodies. At home we filled each box with $10 worth of food, then added $5 to each box to cover the cost of shipping and handling.

For the next year we continued to hear about CHF. In August 2003, my friend Shelene said that she planned to go to Africa with the Children's Hunger Fund that November. Shelene encouraged me to go, but not only did I not have the money, I was also afraid of going due to the migraine headaches I get that can put me in bed for two to three days. They are so debilitating, and I was afraid of getting one over there.

When Shelene returned, she bubbled over with stories about her incredible experience there. She had never experienced anything like this before in her life. The devastation of the children. The love of these children and the joy that they had even though they were the neediest of the needy. With no food, many children were dying of starvation. Sleeping on the dirt, wearing dirty, ripped T-shirts, these children had more joy and appreciation for life than many privileged American children. Shelene informed me that she was going back to Uganda as soon as she could, and that she intended to take me with her.

Shelene stood at my dining room table and fanned out photographs across it. "These children need sponsors," she said. "Without them, they will starve."

I looked at those faces, each one so hungry. "How much?"

"If you can believe it, girlfriend, it's only $30 a month! Each sponsored child gets a uniform and a pair of shoes so they can go to school. They also get to eat—sometimes the only meal they'll get that day."

"The cost of a manicure," I mumbled, my fingers touching each photo. "Of course I'll sponsor one!"

Shelene created a new program in Africa called Jungle Ride that provides bicycles to pastors of small villages so they can go to where the food is being distributed and take it back to share with the village. At the fund-raiser for it I sat mesmerized with the photos, the stories, the need.

Over the course of the next few weeks, changing my mind quite a few times, I decided to go to Africa.

Each time I really thought about my decision and became afraid, Shelene said, "Buddy, who's allowing you to breathe today? Pray about it. He'll take care of it. You'll be fine." If it was God's will for me to go, He would see me through all of my fears and financial considerations.

After much prayer I told her that I would go.

June 20, 2004, I had all my bags packed with toys, clothes, candies—whatever I could stuff inside for the children.

And I woke with a migraine.

I told myself it was just nerves, but after a couple of hours, the intensified pain told me I needed to take my medication.

"You can't go, Barb," Robert said, his eyes reflecting concern.

"I'm going to lay down for one hour. If the migraine isn't gone, then I won't go."

He smiled grimly and nodded.

I went to our darkened bedroom and lay down, thinking there was no way I would be able to fly nine hours to London, and then another nine hours to Uganda. I prayed that if it was God's will for me to go on this trip that He would heal me. I didn't even need to be 100 percent right away, but I had to feel that I could at least get on the plane.

An hour later I woke, sitting up slowly, waiting to feel any sign of the migraine. It was gone. The medication left me feeling a little groggy, but the headache was gone.

I dressed, grabbed my suitcases and called to Robert. "I'm ready! Let's go!"

"Are you sure, Barb? I'm not feeling good about this."

I looked him right in the eye. "I am. And I'm really okay."

When we met Shelene and Brice for the drive to the airport, Robert pulled Shelene aside. He was so worried about me going that he tried to get Shelene to agree that I shouldn't go. Instead, Shelene patted his arm. "She's going to be great, Robert. Really she is."

"What if she gets a migraine while she's there?"

"I'll put her to bed and make her stay. She won't go to the village that day."

Shelene never had to make good on her promise, because I never had a migraine while there. In Africa I felt like I'd come *alive*. All the junk that seemed so important to our lives in America melted in the humidity. In the simplicity. In the poverty. In the joy. Everywhere I went, I saw that the people in these villages understood what life was about. Faith, love, community, sharing.

In the weekly market, where the people go to share their meager wares, Shelene took one of her sponsored children to get her a Coke and a cake. The Cokes come in the old-fashioned bottles, dirty, warm, and the endless flies gathering around the rims. The little girl chose hers, and then bought a muffin that looked old and rather ragged. As she drank the Coke, you'd think she'd been given the greatest prize. Her face registered the pleasure of the worst thirst quenched. As she broke off pieces of her "cake" to eat, other children began to gather, watching her. She broke pieces off for them, handing each one a portion of her prized cake.

"Are these your friends?" Shelene asked.

"No," the girl said. "They're hungry too."

One day, Shelene and I walked through the forest on a dirt path toward a village. We came upon a woman at a makeshift shack built out of a few twigs and banana leaves. She had laid out baked goods that looked somewhat like thick tortillas and warm biscuits.

"How much?"

"One schilling."

"No, for all of it."

Tears filled the woman's eyes as we filled a bag with her entire stock—for about $5.

We had no idea what we would do with the food. We continued our walk toward the village. When we arrived, we both immediately felt for the very pregnant woman who looked ready to deliver. Her eyes bore the weariness of a woman who has no energy left. Yet around her played five children. We looked at her and handed her the food. She began to weep, and passed it out to her eager children.

When I arrived in Gaba, as I stepped off the bus, standing in front of me was a little boy. He looked at me and said, "Kirk is my sponsor."

"Really?" I asked him.

He grinned even bigger, flashing me a priceless smile.

"What is your name?"

"Godfrey," he said, obviously proud of it.

"It's nice to meet you, Godfrey." I opened my arms, and he walked into my hug.

While there, I treated this little boy as if he were another grandchild. Before I left the village, I squatted before Godfrey and said, "When I come back, what would you like me to bring you?"

Without hesitation, Godfrey answered, "A suit."

"A suit?"

"Yes, a suit so I can go to church."

"What color?"

"Blue!" he said, flashing me that brilliant smile.

"Then that's what I will bring you."

Some of the villages were so destitute, the smell of urine everywhere, the filth incomprehensible. I could not fathom all these children living in such unhealthy and horrible living conditions. They didn't have anything, yet they were very grateful to see us coming, hoping for something from us. It didn't matter what we had, children and adults alike wanted whatever it was. I gave an elderly woman aspirin for her arthritis. We gave the children small gifts of stuffed toys.

At one village, one particular boy named Job caught my eye. We connected immediately, and I asked if I could sponsor him.

I came home, not satisfied, but filled with longing to go back, as one often does after a good trip. I wanted to return to see Job and take him some items that would make his life a little easier—clothes and more food.

God, I prayed when I returned, *What can I do to further help these wonderful people?*

God answered in a way that I could not have expected. It came in the form of an invitation from Dave Philips of the Children's Hunger Fund to serve on the board of directors.

No one had ever extended such an invitation to me before. I couldn't imagine how I would be an asset to their board, yet my heart's desire was to serve with this ministry in any way I could. With trembling, I said yes.

The experience has put me right where I want to be—a part of the Children's Hunger Fund. I spread the word wherever I go—dying of hunger is not a disease! There is a cure! CHF is one way to get food and aid to these countries. (And 99.6 percent of the money that comes in to CHF goes to the children and their families.)

Churches can help CHF's Food Pak Program by filling boxes with food and necessary items. CHF picks them up and distributes them throughout the world—not just Africa, but in other countries (including America) where children are living in great poverty and in need of food.

Since my first trip, I have returned to Africa five times. I sponsor two children, Job and Resty. I kept my promise to Godfrey. When I returned the next year, I brought him a black suit with a bright blue shirt, tie, belt, and dress shoes. I have met and photographed many African people (discovering I have a talent for photography!), falling in love with them more and more. Here in the poorest parts of Africa, I've found a purpose to the life God has given me.

chapter 24

Into Life

The seasons of life are amazing things. As this story takes shape on paper, spring is bursting forth its hidden life in the brightest rainbow colors of the flowers and blossoming bushes, as well as the varied greens of the trees that had looked dead—even in our mild California winter. My life has had cycles of these seasons in my heart. And it seems to me that although I am a grandmother many times over, in some ways, this is a new spring season.

After thirty-six years of marriage, Robert and I have settled into an easy rhythm, a way of relating that is kind, generous, romantic, and on occasion, quite tender. Sometimes I find myself still wishing for more—but what woman doesn't? I've embraced my husband fully for who he is, and not who I wish he would be. I've learned to give him the grace I hope he'll give me for being imperfect. He's a good man with strong, moral character, providing faithfully for his family for so many years. True to his word, after retiring in 2004, he spent many hours looking at Scripture, faith and God, finding the repentance and forgiveness I did. It is such a change to now share the most important part of my life with the man I love.

Don't hear me say we've arrived to perfect marital bliss—we haven't! We're still on the journey—but at least we're making it together.

Opposite page: *Bridgette, Melissa and Candace at Melissa's baby shower (January 2006). Bridgette is also pregnant and due a few weeks after Melissa.*

Now retired from thirty-seven years teaching math and physical education at the middle-school level, Robert has remodeled our garage *again*. This time it is a beautiful two-bedroom cottage with hardwood floors and granite countertops. We look forward to what God has planned for this space.

I am yearning to return to Africa. If I could, I would stay for several months at a time, pouring love, help, and food into the lives of these wonderful people. For now, I am satisfied to make trips each year, with my next coming up very soon.

I work for my friend Shelene in her talent development and promotional company once a week, and work at The Way of the Master another day a week. At home I read and answer e-mails from The Way of the Master until the wee hours of the morning. In between, I fill my days with playing tennis and spending time with my children, grandchildren, other family, and friends. My heart is full, and I lack nothing.

After Kirk and Chelsea married on July 20, 1991, the others followed in slow succession. Candace met the man of her dreams on the professional hockey circuit through Dave Coulier. Valeri Bure, a Russian player for the Montreal Canadiens and his brother, Pavel, also a hockey player, had been learning English by watching *Full*

House on television! Sparks flew almost immediately for Candace and Val, but they dated two years before they tied the knot on June 22, 1996 (our anniversary!).

Robert, true to his off-the-norm form, decided the father-daughter dance needed to be a little different than the awkward swaying and stepping on each other's toes affair. So the two of them secretly went to a dance teacher and had their moment choreographed to an eclectic mix of hip-hop, country, and ballroom, taking everyone by complete surprise. It's common knowledge that Robert can't dance, and his remarkable performance showed how hard he had worked. The resultant crowd approval meant that he had to come up with new and unique father-daughter dances when Bridgette married John Ridenour on May 6, 2000, and when Melissa and Jason Fleming married on June 2, 2001. Bridgette and her dad performed a hip-hop routine to *Men In Black*, complete with the trademark sunglasses they'd hidden in their clothes. Melissa was the only daughter to change out of her wedding dress for this dance, donning a red fringed dress number. Melissa and her father, with a red rose in his mouth, captivated the audience as they did complicated dance steps down the Grand Ballroom staircase, finishing their performance with a tango on the dance floor. All three were beyond what anyone ever expected Robert to be able to do. But he performed with the girls like a pro.

Bridgette worked as a stand-in for a total of fifteen years on *Full House* (for Andrea Barber, then Candace), *Home Improvement* (for Jonathan Taylor Thomas), and many commercials and feature films. Being a stand-in is difficult, detail-oriented work. The stand-in must take careful notes on the script to tell the child actor exactly when and where to move, and any script changes, and what's expected of them. The camera operators needed to do light checks and height checks, often having 4'11" Bridgette stand on apple boxes all day. She had to carry them everywhere, finally suggesting they just strap them to her feet.

Bridgette worked as a stand-in on the Disney film *Perfect Game*. One of the grips took notice of her, and made no attempt to hide his flirting. Bridgette, feeling cautious, thought he was cute, and was willing to be friendly, but nothing more. Yet they worked together for a couple of months on the film, interacting daily. Bridgette grew to like him more and more. She came home one day and said, "Mom, this guy asked me out."

"How did you meet him?" I asked casually.

"On the set."

"What does he do?"

"He's a grip."

"Don't do it, Bridgette. Whatever you do, do *not* get involved with a grip."

"Why, Mom? He's nice. There's something about him."

I went on to remind her that he would have to travel a lot on location. If she married him, she'd most likely be sitting at home alone with the children while he was on location—potentially for months at a time.

Bridgette only half listened to me, since this man, John, pursued her gently and persistently until she gave in to his sense of humor and big heart. After ten months, John proposed, and they were married a year later. John has since retired from the entertainment business and has a wonderful job working for the Southern California Gas Company.

Together they have brought into the family three of my grandchildren, Cameron, Everett, and Reese. Bridgette gets to be a

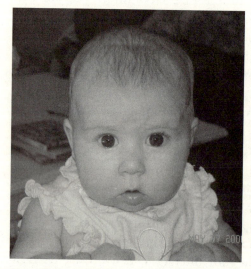 

Kate Helaine (Melissa and Jason's daughter) and cousin Cameron (Bridgette and John's son).

stay-at-home mom to her wonderful kids, living in Indio, California. True to what the psychologist said years ago, Bridgette's is the home where everyone wants to be.

Steady, solid Melissa worked hard waiting tables to put herself through college. She attended California State University of Northridge studying Nutrition and Dietetics. While there, some health issues required her to take a year off. When she returned, she changed her major to Child Development, with a minor in Early Child Care Administration.

Her father cried at her graduation—*his* dream for his children had finally come true for one of them. Robert was so proud of her. For him, this was an accomplishment that was worth more to him than those of the kids who had been on TV.

After college, Melissa continued to wait tables while looking for a job in a related field.

On the first day of Melissa's new restaurant job, all the workers introduced themselves around. "I know you," Jason Fleming said to her.

"How?"

"I'm your friend Allison's boyfriend."

Recognition lit Melissa's mind, remembering Allison had introduced him to her a year before.

As they worked together, talking as coworkers do, they realized they had mutual friends and that Jason had actually gone with those friends to a few Cameron beach Sundays. But that had been years before, and Melissa didn't remember his being there.

After a few months of working together and developing a friendship, Jason confided in Melissa that he planned to break up with Allison. Not too much later he did, then asked Melissa out. Melissa declined, not wanting to get involved with someone right after he had broken up with a serious girlfriend.

But Jason wouldn't take no for a final answer, asking again every so often. It took some time for Melissa to agree to go out with him. However, it didn't take her long to see that Jason was unlike any guy she'd dated. He was gentle, kind, caring, and liked her just as she was. In time, Jason popped the question, and Melissa accepted.

For two years after graduation, Melissa also tried to find a job creating and developing educational toys for infants and toddlers. Not finding what she wanted, but tired of waiting tables, she agreed

to interview for a financial company when a customer invited her to apply. The financial company offered her a job, she accepted, and has been working as a loan processor for three years.

Today, Melissa is happiest as Mommy to darling Kate Helaine, basking in the joy of her new little treasure. She loves being a mother, saying, "Being a mother is by far the best job I have ever had next to being a wife." She, Jason, and Kate live in Canoga Park (just minutes from us). Melissa works part-time out of her home as a loan processor, finding the perfect balance in her world.

After *Growing Pains* had taped its last episode, Kirk pitched a series, titled *Kirk*, about a young college graduate who is chasing his dream of being a superhero illustrator when his aunt takes off, leaving him in charge of his three much younger siblings. *Kirk* also starred Chelsea as a beautiful young woman named Kate, an independent career-driven doctor living across the hall. The show aired for thirty-one episodes (two seasons).

Kirk and Chelsea brought six children into their family. Jack, Isabella, Ahna, Luke, Olivia, and James are loving kids with an array of personalities that would be tough for any parent to keep track of, yet Kirk and Chelsea do, knowing each one and fashioning their discipline and care for them to be as unique as the child. For Kirk, the best part of his life is being the best husband possible to Chelsea and a great father to his kids.

For both Chelsea and Kirk, second closest to their hearts after their children is Camp Firefly, the new name for Camp Callaway. The camp has been in existence since 1989 and still has the same standards as it had the first year. Children no longer come to camp as a result of meeting Kirk on the show, but are picked from choices sent in from children's hospitals and social workers throughout the country who have established a relationship with Kirk and Chelsea over the years. The camp is also dependent upon donations to keep everything running smoothly. Kirk and Chelsea take their children with them each year. This, for them, is the most important and gratifying week of the year for the entire family.

Chelsea has her hands full with caring for the children while Kirk travels to speak at universities, high schools, churches, conferences and community events throughout the country. When he's home, he works on *The Way of the Master*, a reality television show that he and

Left: *The Bure children: Natasha, Lev and Maks (Easter 2005).*
Above: *Olivia, Ahna, and Natasha holding Melissa's baby girl, Kate (April 2005).*

Ray Comfort have created, which won the National Religious Broadcasters' Best Program award for 2005 and 2006 and the People's Choice award for 2004, 2005, and 2006. He also co-hosts The Way of the Master Radio show (which broadcasts daily) and occasionally appears as a guest host for other television shows.

Kirk is still very actively involved in developing family entertainment. He plays the lead role of Buck Williams in three *Left Behind* films, based on the blockbuster novels by Tim LaHaye and Jerry Jenkins. Chelsea plays Hattie in the same films, and has acted with Kirk in the *Growing Pains* reunion movies. Chelsea still enjoys acting—but only if she can take her family with her, and their grandmother and a friend to help watch them.

Kirk's and Chelsea's lives are full. When someone asked Kirk recently if he wanted his children in the business, he said without hesitation, "No way." He clarified that he thoroughly enjoyed his stint in the industry, but that it has changed a lot in the years since he has left, and he wouldn't want his children in that mire. I, for one, cannot imagine trying to shuttle *six* kids to auditions! I had my hands full with three.

Candace and Val Bure live in Florida, where they are raising their three children, Natasha, Lev, and Maksim. Her primary role is in supporting her family and being a mom, but she still does a little acting. Recently she did an episode of the Disney show, *That's So Raven*, because it's her daughter's favorite show. She's also done several E! Entertainment and VH1 specials. Candace is also working with some folks on producing family films. So while family is her first priority, she still dabbles in the entertainment industry, always looking for another way to be a light and share Christ.

Candace also speaks at churches around the country, outreach events for all ages, and Christian colleges. While Val has played professional hockey for twelve years, he developed an interest in real estate, investing in commercial and residential properties. He is a bright man and very business savvy. There is no question that he will succeed in whatever he does once he retires from hockey. But their hearts are really in Russia, Val's homeland. While Russians are a very religious people—churches abound in the vast country—they have no sense of God's Word and knowing Him personally. And because Val grew up in Russia, beginning his notable hockey career there, the Bure name in Russia is the same as Michael Jordan in the States.

What brings Candace the greatest joy is being the best wife and mother she can be. Although her heart still loves acting, she now wants a chance to be in front of people for a different reason: to be able to share her faith with others.

I think what brings me the deepest joy and satisfaction is that all four of my children are leading lives of integrity and faith. All four are great parents in good marriages, living lives that are more than I'd hoped for when they were born. Instead of just being happy, their lives are filled with value and purpose.

During my early years, I had no idea the greater plan God had for me—something much greater than I could have ever imagined. But now as I look back on my life, I can see His fingerprints throughout our lives. I am convinced that He guided us each step of the way. Meeting Robert on the beach that day when I almost didn't go. Putting us in the apartment building with Fran Rich. Giving Kirk the chance to audition, even though we were late. Giving Candace the opportunity to observe her brother so she could learn and feel more comfortable on the set than off. Oh, and so much more. Each step that I thought I was making on my own had Someone far greater whispering in my ear—a voice I later learned to obey. A voice that eventually led me to listen to a CD that brought me into the strong arms of a Savior.

Today I live my life not looking for what I think I deserve, but in humble gratitude for the knowledge that I am saved by grace through faith in the shed blood of Jesus Christ. This is totally a gift—certainly nothing that I deserved or earned. I now desire to live my life according to God's standards of righteousness, not by man's standards of happiness. I know there will be days that I fail, but the days of diving into choosing what I know is wrong and doing it anyway are gone.

Today I don't question the current events in my life. Hopefully there will be many more chapters to come. But one thing I know is that in the final chapter, I will be with Him eternally—forever and ever.

I look forward to experiencing God each day and give thanks for the many blessings in my life. As I walk in obedience and seek to fulfill the Great Commission to go into all the world and preach the gospel to every creature, I pray that I will continue to be the woman, wife, mother, and grandmother He created me to be—and to share what I've learned as the mother of a Full House of Growing Pains.

A full house of grandkids: (front row) Isabella, James, Olivia, Lev, Ahana, Luke, Maks, Natasha, Everett, (back) Cameron and Jack ... plus two more on the way!

Acknowledgments

Thanks to Mom and Dad for your commitment to each other all these years. Thank you for loving me so much. To my mother-in-law Helen, thank you for your love and encouragement with my book.

Thanks to all my sisters for your laughter, sisterhood, and unconditional love. Looking forward to our road trip together! And to my brother Frank for always being there to "protect and to serve."

Mark Spence, thank you for putting the life-changing CD into Kirk's hands.

Ray Comfort, thank you for being a faithful friend. Thank you for the encouragement to write this book and believing there would be someone who would be interested in reading it.

To Lissa Halls Johnson. What can I say, Lissa? When thinking about someone to help me write this book, who would have guessed it was going to be you? After knowing you so many years ago, your coming alongside me today was so unexpected. Thank you for all the many hours of writing, interviewing people, and shaping my book into what it is today. I am truly grateful for your talent and friendship.

To my friend Shelene. Buddy, you have been with me through thick and thin. Thank you for being the wonderful person you are and a sister in Christ. May we continue to bring many more to Africa through the Children's Hunger Fund. Thanks for being my accountability partner in so many areas of my life. You have been such an encouragement to me and I am truly blessed to call you my friend.

To Jono. You have given me so much over the years through being a wonderful friend. Thanks for all the encouragement in helping me with my business. If it hadn't been for you, my agency wouldn't have made it past two years! We had fun during those years of Gravy Train Productions. I will never forget all the fun and laughter along the way!

To Joey Scott. Joey your heart of compassion and love for the "wish kids" was so pure. Thank you for always being there for them. You made them feel so special and went beyond what any other associate producer would have done. Thanks for always being a wonderful friend and helping add so much to my book.

Thank you, Lynn, Judy, and Sara Jay for helping me in the early stages of this book. I know I drove you all crazy! You were a tremendous help to me in getting started. Dale Jackson, thank you for your help and hard work.

Thank you for the Living Waters team who helped out with all the details of this book.

To Jean Young for your encouragement to write this book while we drove the roads of Saboba, Africa.

Thank you, Bob Saget and Jeff Franklin, for taking the time out of your busy schedules to interview with Lissa and for sharing your thoughts about Candace for this book.

Barbara Cameron

No book can be written alone, as much as writers would hope they could.

First, I am thankful to the amazing Barbara Cameron for letting me have the privilege of helping her tell her story. She is more incredible than this book's words could contain, and many of her kind actions and varied accomplishments have had to go without documentation. Her honesty about who she is and what she did is also amazing, considering she is not proud of some of her choices. She is very brave.

Without the input of her family—Robert, Kirk, Bridgette, Melissa, and Candace—I also could not have helped to write this book. Their memories brought delightful details, not to mention a fun family session where I was able to see the loving family dynamics in action. It made me wish I'd been born into this family. The love Barbara wanted for her family is so obvious in the interaction of these tight-knit siblings, as well as in their very funny father.

I also want to thank those who gave me interviews. Every person I spoke with provided me with insight into Barbara and her family that painted a richer picture than they can do of themselves. I was fully aware of the cost of time for these very busy people who gave generously of their memories: Jeff Franklin, creator and showrunner, *Full House*; Sara Getzkin, tutor and friend extraordinaire; Jonathan Koch, President and CEO, Gravy Train Productions; Bob Saget, Danny Tanner on *Full House*; Joey Scott, Producer of *Growing Pains*; and Shelene Bryan, friend.

With special thanks to Beth Cuilla, who provided insight for a very difficult chapter.

I am also grateful to my e-mail group beyond all measure. Your faithfulness made a difference to this book.

And of course, a volume of thanks to my husband, Rich, for his support. This could not have been written without you.

Lissa Halls Johnson

Websites

Barbara Cameron's website: www.barbaracameron.net

How to help hungry children through the Children's Hunger Fund:
www.childrenshungerfund.org

Sponsorship for the children of Uganda, Africa:
www.africarenewal.org

Kirk and Chelsea Cameron's camp for critically ill/terminally ill
children: www.campfirefly.com

Kirk Cameron's website:www.kirkcameron.com

Kirk Cameron's ministries: www.wayofthemaster.com

Ray Comfort's Living Waters Publications: www.livingwaters.com

To hear "Hell's Best Kept Secret":
www.livingwaters.com/learn/hellsbestkeptsecret.htm

Candace Cameron Bure's website: www.candacecameronbure.net

Shelene Bryan's Talent Development:
www.imagedevelopmentonline.com

Melissa Centrella's websites:
www.macscholarship.org (to see a video of Melissa)
www.dystonia-foundation.org

Co-author Lissa Halls Johnson's website:
www.lissahallsjohnson.com

Don't miss "A Full House of Growing Pains" DVD.
For details, go to www.livingwaters.com